W9-CLW-395

About Island Press

Island Press is the only nonprofit organization in the United States whose principal purpose is the publication of books on environmental issues and natural resource management. We provide solutions-oriented information to professionals, public officials, business and community leaders, and concerned citizens who are shaping responses to environmental problems.

Since 1984, Island Press has been the leading provider of timely and practical books that take a multidisciplinary approach to critical environmental concerns. Our growing list of titles reflects our commitment to bringing the best of an expanding body of literature to the environmental community throughout North America and the world.

Support for Island Press is provided by the Agua Fund, The Geraldine R. Dodge Foundation, Doris Duke Charitable Foundation, The Ford Foundation, The William and Flora Hewlett Foundation, The Joyce Foundation, Kendeda Sustainability Fund of the Tides Foundation, The Forrest & Frances Lattner Foundation, The Henry Luce Foundation, The John D. and Catherine T. MacArthur Foundation, The Marisla Foundation, The Andrew W. Mellon Foundation, Gordon and Betty Moore Foundation, The Curtis and Edith Munson Foundation, Oak Foundation, The Overbrook Foundation, The David and Lucile Packard Foundation, Wallace Global Fund, The Winslow Foundation, and other generous donors.

The opinions expressed in this book are those of the author(s) and do not necessarily reflect the views of these foundations.

A Safe and

Sustainable World

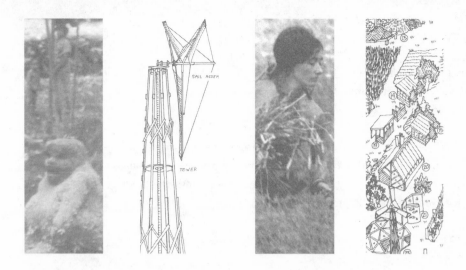

A Safe and Sustainable World

The Promise of Ecological Design

Nancy Jack Todd

PRESS

Washington • Covelo • London

ISLAND PRESS is a trademark of The Center for Resource Economics.

Library of Congress Cataloging-in-Publication data.
Todd, Nancy Jack 1938–
  A safe and sustainable world : the promise of ecological design /
Nancy Jack Todd.
    p. cm
  Includes bibliographical references and index.
  ISBN 1-55963-778-1 (acid-free paper) — ISBN 1-55963-780-3 (pbk. : acid-free paper)
  1. New Alchemy Institute. 2. Ocean Arks International. 3. Environmental protection. 4. Human ecology. 5. Ecological engineering. 6. Sustainable development.
I. Title.
  TD169.T63 2005
  628—dc22
                                                    2004021986

British Cataloguing-in-Publication data available.

Printed on recycled, acid-free paper ♻

Design by Paul Hotvedt, Blue Heron Typesetters

Manufactured in the United States of America
10 9 8 7 6 5 4 3 2 1

For John.

For our children and grandchildren.

For children everywhere. With hope.

Contents

Foreword

David W. Orr

The late 1960s and early 1970s were a time like no other. The complacency and self-congratulation of the 1950s were shattered by the Civil Rights and the Vietnam protest movements, by the constitutional crisis of Watergate, and by the mounting evidence that human tenure on Earth was in jeopardy. Largely unnoticed in the turmoil, a small group of extraordinary scientists and visionaries was rethinking the ecological, material, and philosophical foundations of the modern world. In seminal experiments in southern California and then at the New Alchemy Institute on Cape Cod, a practical, ecological worldview was coming into existence—one powered by sunlight and relying on nature as a partner. This wasn't doom and gloom or back to the caves, as some would have it, but the creation of the necessary components of a prosperous and secure future.

I first heard of the New Alchemy Institute in the early 1970s, and eagerly followed its success. Amidst all of the evidence of ecological degradation, here was hope in the tangible form of bioshelters, "arks," windmills, gardens, and aquatic ecosystems—"elegant solutions predicated on the uniqueness of place," as John Todd put it. While many were focused on stopping one thing or another, the New Alchemists were starting to create workable models of sustainability long before that word became common. For scientists, the legacy of the New Alchemy Institute and its successor, Ocean Arks International, is interesting and important for what it says about the role of nature as a model for human-made systems. For educators, the work of the New Alchemists is interesting and important as a model of learning based on the creative assembly of life forms, not dissection and reduction. The New Alchemists studied and experimented as if we did indeed "live in the lap of great intelligence," as Emerson once thought. Their work aimed to draw on that reservoir of wisdom by integrating food, shelter, waste cycling, and energy technologies within the larger patterns and harmonies of the natural world.

The partnership of John Todd, the scientist, and Nancy Jack Todd, artist, dancer, and writer, is itself a beautiful and important part of this story, a union of science and art. This may explain their great success in making bioshelters, arks, wastewater systems, pond restorers, and living machines not merely functional and interesting but also works of art that celebrate water and life, that speak to our imagination and our hearts as strongly as to our intellect.

These pages tell the history of the New Alchemy Institute up to a point, but the rest of the story is yet to unfold. We face looming challenges of biotic impoverishment, climate change, the end of the era of cheap portable fossil fuels, and the threat of terrorism brought on in no small part by our profligate use of energy and materials and the consequent necessity to protect our sources of supply at whatever cost to whomever. That effort can only end badly and perhaps catastrophically. The work of the New Alchemists, Ocean Arks International, and others continues to show that we could make a different world, one safer, fairer, more prosperous, more secure, and far more decent. It is axiomatic in a commercial culture to take more than you give. The lesson of the New Alchemists, on the contrary, is the ancient truth that the gift must move and that we live by the grace of a benevolence that evolved over the ages on a beautiful water planet powered by the charity of sunshine.

Acknowledgments

It would be virtually impossible to give appropriate credit to the hundreds of people whose work and ideas were pivotal to the developments recounted in this book. The list would be many pages long, and even then some people would inevitably be overlooked. Both New Alchemy and Ocean Arks have been the shared vision of many people over the years. Many of the same people are today counted among the growing ranks of those who make up the global movement for peace, justice, and environmental sustainability—a force that the *New York Times* has called the world's other superpower.

I doubt that I could have undertaken this writing in the first place if Hilde Maingay and Earle Barnhart had not had the vision and the perseverance to reclaim the place that had been New Alchemy and give it a story with a happy ending. Alchemy Farm and the restored Ark, which is now part of their solar home, are a symbol of and enduring testimony to all that we worked for. I am additionally indebted to Earle for making his collection of the *New Alchemy Quarterly* available to me for reference, and for his daring arboreal feat in obtaining the aerial photographs of the Ark and his house as they now stand.

I also drew on the old *Journals* and other New Alchemy publications and reports, as well as Ocean Arks' *Annals of Earth,* as sources for most of the information recorded here. They were supplemented by the recollections of many friends, including Bill McLarney, Susan Ervin, Christina Rawley, Ron Zweig, John Quinney, Colleen Armstrong, and Michael Shaw. For technical assistance in the areas of energy and computer modeling, I have relied on Tyrone Cashman, Greg Watson, Gary Hirshberg, John Quinney, and Al Doolittle. All of them have been patient and helpful. John Todd was equally so in checking over the scientific material. The steadfast friendships of Colleen Armstrong, Denise Backus, Susan Ervin, Christina Rawley, and Kathi Ryan have kept the spirit of New Alchemy alive for me. Sue and Jim Condon have been behind the project throughout, providing the occasional necessary distraction to revitalize my resolve.

Camilla Humphrey provided much needed advice on my first unwieldy attempt at a manuscript. This leads me to reiterate my explanation to the hundreds of people who took part in New Alchemy over the years who are not specifically mentioned. The earlier drafts of the book were so all-inclusive of names and projects as to be bewilderingly incomprehensible. They read as much like a roll call as a narrative. It was Joan Pearlman who led me to the realization that I had written my first version for the New Alchemists and their friends. My challenge, as she pointed out at the time, was to write it for everyone else.

Still pondering how to distill what was truly important from the massive maze of information available, it occurred to me that at the core of it all was what the research and experience of New Alchemy and Ocean Arks have taught us, what we learned that could be of use to the world in its current state. This, while greatly simplifying the telling, necessitated omitting naming many of the individual contributors who deserve honoring. For that I am truly sorry. I should also add that even after talking to many of those involved over the years, I could write this account only from my own perspective. There could well be as many other possibilities as there were New Alchemists and Ocean Arkers.

Finally, my heartfelt thanks go to Barbara Dean for her supportive response to the manuscript, and to my editor, Heather Boyer, for her invaluable and insightful guidance in honing my rambling account into this book.

Introduction

"There is something infinitely healing," declared Rachel Carson, in her 1956 book, *The Sense of Wonder*, "in the repeated refrains of nature, the assurance that dawn comes after night, and spring after winter." There is literally "something infinitely healing" in the dynamics of the natural world, perhaps in more dimensions than Rachel Carson implied in her book. For more than thirty years a number of scientists and their colleagues have made the study of Carson's "refrains of nature" in the form of ecosystems, great and small, the focus of their research. Their goal was to decode the processes that give rise to the resiliency and robustness of those systems and to ascertain their role in maintaining the continuity of life on Earth. Their hope in doing so was to learn whether and how the interrelationships among living organisms, ranging from microorganisms, to terrestrial and aquatic plants, to higher animals, might help us to solve the daunting environmental problems we confront in the early twenty-first century.

Neither a litany nor an analysis of the potentially catastrophic environmental threats looming on the horizon is the subject of this book. Suffice it to note that in 1994 more than 1,600 scientists—104 of them Nobel Laureates—issued the World Scientists' Warning to Humanity. It declared unequivocally: "Human beings and the natural world are on a collision course. . . . If not checked many of our current practices put at serious risk the future that we wish for human society and the plant and animal kingdoms, and may so alter the living world that it will be unable to sustain life in the manner we know."

Educator and author David Orr succinctly summarized what is at stake in his 1994 book, *Earth in Mind*: "The problem is simply how a species pleased to call itself *Homo sapiens* fits on a planet with a biosphere." As the effects of phenomena like global warming become apparent, the current answer to Orr's question is "Not very well." Many years ago Ramona Peters of the Wampanoag tribe on Cape Cod articulated the dilemma in another way. She was contrasting the ancestral traditions of the Wampanoag with the exploitive and destructive technologies of advanced industrial economies. "My people don't understand you," was the gist of her message. "We don't understand why you are still trying to take our land; why you must always have more of everything. A seed—a flower—a tree unfolds according to the instructions it has been given. As a people we have always tried to live according to our own instructions. We don't understand what *your* instructions are."

Again there is no easy answer. For corporate-driven, industrial/electronic cultures, an understanding of how we are to live amid the vast complexity of the natural world is long forgotten—or ignored. Yet the Greek myth of Pandora reminds us that even when, by dint of unrestrained human curiosity and meddling, all the evils had been let loose in the world, hope still remained in the bottom of the box. So, too, in our time.

This is the story of a number of people who banded together in the simple but heartfelt hope that humanity could one day live free of the shadow of the environmental apocalypse of which the World Scientists warned. In doing so we found ourselves embarking on a search for what Ramona Peters called our "instructions." Finding workable alternatives to what the World Scientists referred to as "current practices" was the focus of a small research and education institute called New Alchemy and its subsequent offshoot, Ocean Arks International.

When my husband, John Todd, our friend Bill McLarney, and I founded the New Alchemy Institute in 1969, no one knew whether it would ever be possible to provide sustainably, over time, for the planet's human population. Now, as the result of our own work, in conjunction with that of thousands of other individuals and groups, we not only know that this is possible, but we also know how to do it. In addition, we have learned that scarred landscapes and polluted waters can be healed. In doing so, we have uncovered many of the necessary building blocks for creating sustainable, lasting cultures. It is within our reach, again quoting David Orr from his 2002 book, *The Nature of Design*, "to remake the human presence in the world."

We now know that it is not beyond human understanding to coevolve toward a relationship of respect and reciprocity with the natural systems of Earth, a relationship based not on exploitation but on an informed love of place and planet. This book is an account of the trials and errors incurred in first thinking through and then substantiating this relationship. It is traced through the history of New Alchemy and Ocean Arks, and the people, places, technologies, and ideas these institutes have spawned, culminating in the emerging field of ecological design. It is also a recollection of the individual and institutional struggles encountered in our quest for what the far-sighted ecologist Gregory Bateson once summarized as "a paradigm with a future."

Gregory Bateson made that pronouncement about New Alchemy's work almost thirty years ago. Although the intervening times have seen enormous changes, especially in the area of technology, that paradigm with a future is not yet the operating principle determining either government or economic policy.

Sooner or later, however, it is a matter of survival that some form of ecological consciousness guide the behavior of significant numbers of people. As author and environmental activist Paul Hawken has predicted, the tenets of sustainability must ultimately prevail because they arise from an empirical, scientifically verifiable understanding of the planet's finite life support systems.

That an understanding of the ramifications of an ecological worldview has yet to take hold is a phenomenon I can understand. Human as opposed to environmental causes have always come more readily to me. It was in living through the experiences recounted here that I became a deeply committed advocate of ecologically based, environmentally benign ways of living. That, in essence, is what led to my writing this book. Through studying and working with people dedicated to finding a path to lighten our individual and collective impact on Earth, I have come to an understanding of the world that, for me, is scientifically accurate and profoundly satisfying intellectually, aesthetically, and spiritually. It is an understanding that contains seeds of honest hope and is a worldview I am convinced should be more widely understood.

The book begins with a brief retrospective of John Todd's early research in biology and the way his discoveries affected our thinking. Equally pivotal to our future direction was the emerging environmental movement of the late 1960s. A more immediate catalyst was the academic restriction of that time, which led three not otherwise drastically radical people to step outside the mainstream and found our own institute. After we had found a site on Cape Cod and the work was under way, we began to define our complex quest for more sustainable ways of living as research into alternative, environmentally sound methods for providing basic human needs. We further divided this still challenging and amorphous mandate into intensive experiments in food, energy, and shelter, each of which is covered in the early chapters. After several years of research, and having in the main a fine time while we were at it, we were ready to integrate the results of what we had learned into experiments in large, ecologically designed solar greenhouses that became known as bioshelters. This in turn led to a series of interdisciplinary discoveries in the dynamics of ecosystems and their application to solving human problems. This work continues into the present.

As the credibility of New Alchemy's early work was becoming established, Bill McLarney transplanted many of the ideas to Costa Rica to establish a comparable institute there. Later John Todd and I founded Ocean Arks International with the dual intentions of taking the work farther out into the world and pushing the research in the direction of environmental restoration. More recently many of the tenets and practices of ecological design have begun penetrating mainstream thinking and policy and have evolved a significant economic dimension. Though widely scattered now, the people involved in both New Alchemy and Ocean Arks have continued to practice their ideals and to influence their communities, urban and rural, national and global, in their commitment to their "paradigm with a future." This period is the subject of the concluding chapters.

My wish in retelling these experiences is to invite readers to join with us in discovering the knowledge, methodologies, technologies, and mind-set that emerged along the way. Fundamental to that journey is the underlying understanding that the instructions as to how human cultures are to live lie encoded in the living systems of our unique and irreplaceable home planet.

chapter one

How It All Began

Never doubt that a small group of thoughtful, committed
people can save the world. Indeed, nothing else ever has.
—Margaret Mead

How to pinpoint the beginnings of an idea, to say with certainty what
started us on our search for our "instructions"? What was to become
the New Alchemy Institute was unquestionably a logical outgrowth of
its time, of the social, political, and environmental tumult of the late
1960s, '70s, and '80s. Its origins equally can be traced to the childhood
experiences of its three founders: John Todd, Bill McLarney, and myself.

As a boy John had been devastated by the post–World War II industrial development that was invading the farmlands, woods, and
marshes near his home on the north shore of Lake Ontario. Disturbed
at seeing him so visibly unhappy, his understanding parents introduced
him to books on agriculture, forestry, conservation, and restoration.
From his reading John learned that it was possible to restore polluted
and barren lands and waters and to reverse and heal the tide of destruction. This launched him on a lifelong voyage of discovery.

Bill McLarney was born across Lake Ontario from John in the town
of Randolph in upstate New York. His mother was a teacher. Her love
of books and reading instilled in him a keen ear for language. Lengthy
fishing excursions with his yarn-spinning father bred in him a love of
tall tales and an affinity for the natural world. Growing up in a small
town, with its give-and-take and tolerance of eccentricity, gave him a
sense of place and community that few members of his own, or of succeeding, generations have known. Like John, he mourned the passing
of such a feeling of belonging.

I was born in South Africa of Canadian parents. Our family traveled extensively throughout my childhood. Wherever we found ourselves, my parents managed to create a secure sense of home for my younger sister, Barbie, and me through stories, games, and Sunday expeditions to the country. Yet even the closeness of our family circle could not shelter us from the echoes of World War II. Hitler was the bogeyman of our childhood nightmares. Barbie and I watched adults huddle around the radio as though it were an oracle. We overheard stories of valiant young men shot down over Germany and of children whose fathers would never come home to them again. I became haunted by a horror of war and violence until, at some point, I began to nurture a stubborn hope for a world where such things would not have to happen.

John and I met in Canada while we were still in high school. Even then we were caught up in the ideas that were to form the rest of our lives. As we rambled the Ontario countryside together, John envisioned how the run-down farms we saw could be made productive again. I talked to him of the ban-the-bomb and anti-nuclear movements in England as I puzzled over how I too could find a way to stand up for what I believed in. When John went to off McGill University's Macdonald Agricultural College in Montreal, I stayed at home to study liberal arts at the University of Western Ontario. We weathered the years of partial separation and were married when I graduated. John continued on at McGill and took a master's degree in tropical medicine and behavioral science.

In the late 1960s we moved to Ann Arbor for John to study for his doctorate in biology at the University of Michigan. It was there we met his fellow graduate student Bill McLarney, young, lean, perennially hungry, and harboring passions for fish, jazz, and the tropics. John and Bill spent their days in the lab in the basement of the School of Natural Resources, where John was studying the social behavior of fishes. I elected to stay at home with our children—we had two by then—discovering and delighting in the unfolding of young minds and personalities. John and I were equally fascinated with observing the behavior of our respective charges. Years later we confessed that privately we each had thought our own pursuits much more interesting and that the other had been a bit deluded. Bill was just as involved in his own research on fish in their natural environment, part of which seemed to require long hours of lying facedown at the edge of a stream, eyes trained toward the bottom on the off chance that one of his catfish might move. They rarely did, but when we went along, it made for a fine afternoon of idling.

In those years the war in Vietnam cast a shadow over everyone's life in one way or another. Ann Arbor was a hub of the protest movement, and I joined Ann Arbor Women for Peace. Many evenings, once John got home from the lab, I left the children with him and headed off to one of the countless meetings, lectures, or demonstrations demanding an end to the war. As was to become a custom with us, John, Bill, and I frequently discussed the ramifications of what each of us was doing. They were both deeply committed to their science and felt more divided than I did when critics of the war questioned the neutrality of science and its role in inflicting suffering and death. At times we speculated on the possibility of redirecting scientific research toward nurturing, restoring, and healing both people and the environment. It was an idea that stayed with us.

By 1969 Bill and John and I and our children had moved to San Diego. Bill and John, armed with their newly minted PhDs, were teaching and doing research at San Diego State College. At that time concern for the environment was fast gaining momentum. There were no peace groups nearby, so, wanting to learn more about environmental issues, John and I began to hold informal evening seminars in our living room. We invited students, researchers, and other speakers to present papers on some aspect of the overall problem. The talk would often last long into the night, well after the formal presentations were over and most of the people had gone home—sometimes leaving just John, Bill, and me. We would linger, exhausted, discussing the ramifications of whatever environmental horror story we had heard earlier. One question arose repeatedly: Could anything be done? And if so, what?

My anxiety was compounded by a sinking fear for the future of our children. By that time I was pregnant with our third baby. The smog in San Diego was not as bad as in Los Angeles, but on most days an ominous band of rusty yellow could be seen on the rim of the blue California sky. It was said to be caused by lead fallout from car exhaust and was thought to affect brain development in children. Whenever one of our children seemed less alert than normal, I worried that their brains might be showing symptoms of lead damage. As my sense of urgency grew, I resolved to alert others. I wrote beseeching letters to friends, administrators, officials, newspapers, to anyone I thought might pay attention, because I knew that for my own children to have a future, it had to be secured for all children. Looking back, I realize that was the beginning of my slowly dawning awareness of humanity's utter dependence on the biological life-support systems of the natural world. I had come to understand how ineluctably and inextricably intertwined with my own life and the lives of those I love are the multifold life-forms, from bacteria to sparrow to giant redwood, of the natural world, of the planet.

My anxiety was not fermenting in isolation. In San Diego, environmental concern was becoming a groundswell. Plans for the first Earth Day were under way, and John and Bill were becoming involved in the more public arena. They were being asked to give talks not only at the college but at a series of rallies, conferences, and meetings. At one Ecology Action gathering, in classic McLarney style, Bill told his listeners, "I enjoy nature, but it relaxes me less and less. Today, when I go for a hike in the woods or lie on a beach, I have the uneasy feeling of sitting up with a sick friend. I still enjoy her company, but the fact of her illness—and the uncertainty of the prognosis—introduces an element of tension into the relationship." Reporting on one of John's talks in which he urged that "people investigate new lifestyles that respect all life," the *San Diego Street Journal and Free Press* proclaimed "Todd Speech Highlights State Ecology Conference."

There were two more experiences that substantiated our concerns and determined the direction of the research at what was to become New Alchemy well before the institute actually became a working entity. Looking back, it becomes obvious that our thinking over the years was catalyzed by a series of formative discoveries of the kind that are symbolized in comic strips by a flashing lightbulb. The first of these "Aha!" experiences grew out of one of John's experiments while we were still in Ann Arbor. For months in his lab he had been observing the interactions of social species of fish such as bullheads or catfish in large tanks. Watching their interactions over time, he began to believe there must be some form of communication taking place among the members of the community. The fish behaved as though they were sending and receiving signals. He concluded that information was being exchanged by means of a finely tuned system that operated through their sense of smell and that they maintained social order through olfactory signals. The results formed the basis of his doctoral thesis and later were published in the journal *Science*.

In a follow-up experiment after we moved to San Diego, John documented what happened when brown bullheads (*Ictalurus nebulosis*) were exposed to pollutants. His findings were extremely disturbing. Minute administrations of DDT, for example, did not kill the fish outright. The effect rather was to jam the signals of those communication systems he had documented at the University of Michigan. The DDT was unraveling ancient, evolved patterns of behavior. With their olfactory communication chemically disrupted, the social hierarchy of the bullhead community broke down. Unprecedented outbreaks of aggression occurred. Parents ate their young. The chemicals were affecting not only the physical health of individuals but also the social stability of the community. It did not take a great leap of the imagination to wonder what the steady infusion of industrial and agricultural chemicals into the environment was doing to other life-forms, ourselves included. John learned that other like-minded biologists and lay observers were reporting comparable dislocations among other species. He commented at the time: "It struck us that what we were observing indicated that humanity was reversing ecological processes on a global scale. To continue to ignore these biological lessons may prove, in the long run, a little bit like serving cyanide to the pilot of an aircraft while pouring champagne for the passengers. Fun for a while, but not exactly adaptive."

Our second pivotal Aha! experience took place not in the lab, but in the dry, hilly countryside southeast of the city, where John and Bill were taking their biology students from San Diego State on a series of field trips. I went along with the kids for the pure pleasure of letting them run free in the open country. Besides providing a fine excuse for glorious outings, these trips produced the next discovery that was to chart our course. The stated purpose of the excursions was to involve students in direct contact with a local ecosystem. There was another less official reason. Friends of ours, attracted by the back-to-the-land movement, had rented a ranch just north of the U.S.–Mexico border, intending to homestead. They were happy to have the class wander freely about the place but hoped that as a result of our forays we might be able to teach them how to support themselves on the land without destroying it. We were eager to help and regularly fanned out over the terrain.

Our expectations dimmed quickly. The rambling hills that stretched to the horizon beneath vast reaches of bright sky were composed of dry, sandy grit. They gave rise to chaparral, manzanita bushes, boulders, and the occasional live oak but not much else. There seemed to be no tillable soil. We could not find a source of water. We became discouraged. We had to admit we had no idea what our friends should do. Then John decreed the problem was that we did not know enough; that we could not, in his words, "read the landscape." For all the advanced degrees and theoretical and biological education among us, we had no idea of how to go about supporting ourselves in this arid environment. Unlike the long-vanished native peoples, we academics did not know how to find food or water or where to plant crops. We did not know how to survive there.

This initiated a second phase. We would ask the land, we decided, to teach us what we needed to know. Every student was assigned one element of the environment to study in detail, then to teach the rest of us what he or she had learned. Soil and soil animals, insects, reptiles, plants, shrubs, rocks, trees, birds, and animals were either noted or collected, studied, and catalogued. Everyone made extensive notes and compared discoveries. Slowly a few patterns became discernible. Beyond the site's obvious potential for wind and solar power, we were uncovering more subtle clues. Midway up a small gorge, for example, we found a plant, the roots of which are known to seek moisture. We began to think that somewhere nearby there must be a hidden spring. Below this, where the gorge began to flatten out, there was a live oak tree and an association of plants that included miner's lettuce, which, we learned, required good soil. Once we had stumbled on clues for a water source and tillable soil, a garden became a possibility. If our friends were to dig fishponds and install a water-pumping windmill to link the pond and gardens, they could have the beginnings of an agricultural ecosystem.

We had begun to crack the code and the prospects unfolded enticingly. Then, sadly, the story came to an abrupt end. As excitement began to stir, their landlady arrived from the city and announced to our gentle, long-haired friends that she was raising the rent. They argued, but she was adamant. The increase was much more than they could afford, and they were forced off the land. Even before they had departed, bulldozers appeared on the horizon to level not only their dreams but the ground itself for another outcrop of California weekend houses. What we took away with us was a rueful realization of our ignorance of the real world and an awakened awareness of the profound resources available in looking to nature as our teacher.

New Alchemy Is Born

Through all this mix of inputs John, Bill, and I continued to piece together disparate bits of information, striving for a more comprehensive understanding of the social/environmental dynamic. It was not long before the administration at San Diego State recognized that John was emerging as a leader in the environmental field. In the spring of 1970, he was named associate dean of science and head of a soon-to-be-established department of environmental studies. It proved a short-lived appointment. As John mapped out the courses and the projects he considered essential to further grapple with the dynamics of ecology, he found there was a college regulation prohibiting almost all of them. There was not then, as there is now at many universities, the flexibility within established institutions to permit the cross-disciplinary studies or fieldwork to investigate the basics of sustainability he envisioned. Environmental studies was a more limited field and little to no attention was given to possible countermeasures to the pollution and depletion of natural resources that was motivating us. John decided he could not accept the appointment.

The kind of sweeping change we felt necessary was far too radical for the academic world at that time. Furthermore, while both John and Bill fully honored the importance of documenting environmental trends, they knew that they did not want to spend their lives engaged in what they came to call doomwatch biology. They, and I, felt strongly drawn in another direction—to a quest for viable alternatives to the prevailing dynamic. It was then that we knew the time had come for us to strike out on our own and create our own organization.

The decisive moment came late one night when, after much soul-searching, we asked one another, "Is it too late? Does one of us—or anyone more knowledgeable—have compelling evidence that it is useless to make an effort, however tenuous, to swim against the mainstream of unchecked technological and corporate exploitation that is causing most of the environmental destruction?" None of us had reached that point of hopeless resignation. So we began to focus on what might be done. Was it, in fact, possible to support Earth's population over time while protecting the natural world? And if so, how?

One thing we were sure of. The project was bigger than the three of us. We would have to join forces with others who shared our views. Perhaps we could form a group? We could band together with other interested people and explore ideas—some traditional, some untried—that would help us learn whether and how we could live more sustainably. We did half realize the monumental nature of what we were about to attempt. Yet we knew we had to try. We felt somehow called upon by our time. Asian scholars might say we were following the Tao— the way of nature, a path connecting human intelligence with the resilience of 3.8 billion years of Earth's evolution.

John and I spent months casting about for a name for our fledgling group. We mulled over a number of unwieldy candidates. The Institute for Adaptive Technologies? Biological Restoration? Bioremediation? Applied Ecology? All sounded ponderous and lacked poetry. Then one night, for no accountable reason, John suggested, "New Alchemy?" Somehow we knew at once that it was right, although it was only after extensive reading that we came to understand traditional alchemy as the ancient and honorable discipline it was, a metaphor through which practitioners sought to discover hidden meanings beyond the apparent surfaces and workings of the visible world.

The greatest relevance of alchemy for us was its potential for transformation. This traditionally was symbolized by the philosopher's stone, representing the transmutation, purification, and redemption of matter. So with our own reincarnation of alchemy, we saw it as our mission to transform not only ourselves but our understanding and behavior in relation to the natural world. Writing of the relationship between traditional alchemy and New Alchemy, poet Betty Roszak noted that the alchemists of old had worked "to awaken the dormant powers of nature, to reconcile her dynamic conflicts, and to assist at the birth of a new and higher consciousness." She concluded: "If there are those like the New Alchemists who can restore this forgotten sacred vision to our impoverished awareness, then there is hope for the renewal of the earth."

In referring to the "dormant powers of nature," Betty Roszak understood perfectly what we intended to do. John subsequently reported in one of our first newsletters:

The New Alchemy Institute was formally organized in 1969 after a decade of discussions and gatherings on the part of a small group of scientists, artists, and humanists. The goals of the New Alchemists are both biological and social. As ecologists we are carrying out research in agriculture, aquaculture, power generation, and other fields aimed at enabling humanity to satisfy its needs without destroying the resources that provide them. Where the environment has already been scarred and partially destroyed, we wish to heal and restore it, to make the Earth and its people sing again.

Having taken that first and giant step of naming our fledgling undertaking and beginning to articulate its mission, the next phase in our institutional progression from talk to embodied entity began. As if electing to labor under an unorthodox name were not challenge enough, we went on to adopt the credo: "To restore the land, protect the seas, and inform the Earth's Stewards." And however pretentious or absurdly quixotic it sounded, it was utterly heartfelt: the very broadest interpretation of our transformational mission.

Continuing its long march from idea to legal institute, New Alchemy was incorporated and received its status as a tax-exempt, nonprofit organization in California in June 1970. John was president and I was vice president. The ultimate responsibility for what still seemed ridiculous to call an institute lay with a board of directors, which was made up of John, Bill, and me, and our California lawyer. The advantage to having obtained a legal identity was that it enabled us to begin to look for financial support and to launch a membership program to help us do so. We offered membership to individuals and groups who could contribute financially as well as to those willing to work on some of the early projects. This also marked the beginning of what was always to be the Sisyphean challenge of fund-raising. John had predicted fairly accurately, "The main sources of support for the New Alchemy Institute will be granting agencies and the contributions of the association's members. It is our intention to keep our costs as low as possible by eliminating frills and by purchasing equipment built to last. Much of our work is and will be done by volunteers and the salaries of our paid staff will be conservative. We measure the quality of our lives by our work and our associations, not by our possessions."

He went on to call for the development of "pure energy for powering the communities of the future, experimental and teaching centers, and a New Alchemy Knowledge Center." The call for pure energy voiced the dangers of dependency on nuclear and fossil fuels and advocated the development of renewable sources such as solar, tide, and wind. Communities, John wrote, should be "sustainable and appropriate to ecosystems in which they are located. Structures should be simple and derived from the local landscape."

A Transcontinental Shift

In the summer of 1970, in the midst of all this conceptualizing, organizing, and planning, John and Bill accepted positions at the Woods Hole Oceanographic Institution on Cape Cod. John and I and the kids drove across the country in a Volkswagen camper to arrive on the Cape in early July. In spite of a number of adventures that involved circumventing Woodstock en route, Bill was not far behind us. Homesteading was still very much in the air, and we embraced it as another pillar of our ideals. John and I bought a small, shingled house on an acre and a half of land that was surrounded by woods and only a short walk to the sea, and I sank deep, deep roots for the first time in my life. It is still home. Like many other families at the time, we planted fruit trees and raised chickens and grew vegetables.

At that stage New Alchemy was still largely a paper reality. Anyone who started an organization in the dark ages before e-mail will readily understand this. Excited letters, mostly supportive and helpful, flew back and forth. Some contained modest financial contributions. We rented a small office in the town of Falmouth, not far from our house, where we wrestled with the expanding flow of correspondence and wrote and published the first *New Alchemy Newsletter*. That first winter, retired air force lieutenant colonel Bob Angevine, who had served in Korea and Vietnam, came on as our business manager as well as a board member. He took over most of the internal financial administration from John. He saw his job of overseeing the activities of his idealistic charges as the unusual challenge it was, and enjoyed it.

Beyond the office, New Alchemy was still mainly in its household phase. Our so-called institute was then a nascent and unstructured collection of people engaged in experiments in backyard gardens and fish tanks. One winter Bill created an amazing watery and leaky labyrinth made up of children's swimming pools, buckets, and tubes for a fish-growing experiment in the basement of his winter rental. When it had to be hastily dismantled with the unexpectedly early return of the owners, the argument for a more satisfactory and permanent workplace had been made.

We were having a fine time that first year on the Cape, adjusting once again to more pronounced changes in the seasons, the shorter growing period, and the brooding, gray-brown winters. Although we had not originally intended to establish a permanent New Alchemy center here, we had settled in. John and Bill still had their jobs at Woods Hole Oceanographic and, somewhat frantically, were dividing their time. The children were in school, and I had fallen in love with the Cape's sensual summers, the woods, and the omnipresence of the sea. It was becoming clear that we were here to stay. One of our many visitors at that time was

The first New Alchemy dome in the Todds' front yard, with Susannah Todd at the door.

Richard Merrill, whom we knew by reputation as one of California's foremost teachers and practitioners of organic agriculture. We found we had an enormous amount in common, and he agreed to return the following summer to help us get our agricultural program off to a good start.

Even without an organizational center as such, people were gravitating to the ideas. Somehow they were in the air. One day a young architect from Cambridge called offering to put up a geodesic dome—then considered very hip. John and I volunteered our front yard as venue. The Cambridge people appeared, and, on our end, a work crew made up of an unpredictable combination of friends and people unknown to us until then materialized. And so, in the course of a summer Sunday afternoon in 1971, as children ran and shouted and adults worked and talked, sustained on infusions of beer, we had our first New Alchemy dome raising. We later installed a children's swimming pool in the middle of the clear-sided structure, added fish, and planted the circumference with flowers, herbs, and vegetables. The salad crops grew so luxuriantly one young enthusiast allowed that he would like to be able to duck in, spray on a little dressing, and graze. From working in the dome and our other experiments in gardening and fish raising we were on a strong learning curve. From our correspondence and expanding network we felt the momentum of the ideas growing.

Landfall

As all this was unfolding, it was becoming painfully clear that New Alchemy had outgrown its paper, legal legitimization, and household phases. What was sorely lacking was a physical center that would both consolidate and ground the ideas. We had not intended to establish a center on the Cape—it was less than ideal for our purposes in many ways. For all the Cape's charm, it is far from rural. It was and is a woodsy suburbia, then rapidly developing and now sadly over the mark. Yet there we were. And by that time, in order to achieve full legitimacy in our own eyes as well as the eyes of our supporters—and critics—New Alchemy had to become a place where you could go and see for yourself how the ideas were being manifested, where you could ask questions and get your hands dirty or your feet wet in a fish pond. All this prompted us to begin searching in earnest for land nearby. Word reached us of a possibility, an old dairy farm about 7 miles from our house. The owners proved sympathetic to our ideas and were willing to rent it to us. Negotiations proceeded amicably, and we signed a lease in the late fall of 1971.

For Bill, Cape Cod was to be home for only part of the year. Long drawn to the tropics, his star was to guide him to Costa Rica, where he founded his own organization to explore the potential for sustainable living. Bill had visited Costa Rica in 1968 and had succumbed completely to the country's beauty and its people. He had made a few contacts on that first trip and thought that it would be as good a place as any to test some of his ideas. And as he was to find repeatedly, although conditions in Costa Rica may have been less dire than elsewhere, there were still enough problems to keep one ecologically minded, Spanish-speaking, fish-loving gringo and his colleagues gainfully employed for many years. He was there, he once explained, because he felt it was where he could do the most good. In 1971 the New Alchemy Institute Sociedad Anomima (Incorporated), first known as NAISA, later as the Asociación ANAI, was recognized as a legal entity. Bill has since spent part of every year there.

For the rest of us, the Farm, as we always referred to it, was to be home to New Alchemy for the duration of its working life. We now had access to 12 sandy acres that were a patchwork of overgrown fields and woods. As the old farm had been a dairy operation, we had acquired, in addition to the old farmhouse, a truly capacious barn with a small apartment in an upper corner. At this point we still had only two paid staff members, who were mainly involved in administrative work. Everyone else worked at other jobs as well. We took care of physical maintenance of the house and land ourselves with the help of volunteers and friends. With the move onto the land, we knew that the time to test our rhetoric had come. To transpose

The dome building crew: *Left to right,* Dave Engstrom; Jim Maingay; Hilde Maingay with her three sons; the Cambridge architects, Fred (Multi) Facet and Marsha Zillis; Bill McLarney; friends Laurie Stein and Annie Hinds; and the Todds. *Extreme left,* Bill McLarney in pursuit of a butterfly.

so much that had been theoretical into the tangible, to materialize the ideas that might decode our instructions, was the next challenge before us.

It was a challenge we embraced eagerly. We were to find that our first summer on the land established a pattern, flowing from day to day, that was to set the basic rhythms of our work for the life span of the Institute. The Farm rapidly became a magnet, drawing scores of visitors, and, to our amazement, we were inundated with offers of help from volunteers from the community and summer visitors to Cape Cod. The presence of Rich and Yedida Merrill was critical. They shared New Alchemy's interest in an ecological agriculture that was not only organic but integrated with aquaculture, worm culture, beehives, livestock, and recycled wastes. They teemed up with Hilde Maingay, who was emerging as a leader in our own garden. This freed John to concentrate, with Bob Angevine, more on administration and fund-raising and, with Bill, to experiment in aquaculture. While all of us, children included, took part to some degree in everything that was going on—from building domes to composting, gardening, aquaculture, publishing, and administration—this was the division of generalization and specialization that framed our basic infrastructure and informal division of labor for many years.

By this stage New Alchemy was many things. Legally and accurately we described ourselves as a small, nonprofit research and education institute. We were also a working collective, a group of close friends with a shared vision, and a loosely structured collaborative of environmental activists. We made all important decisions at a weekly meeting. Group decisions were reached through a process of lengthy discussions and consensus. Attendance was compulsory, as the meetings were essential to our functioning as a group. Meetings could be interesting, agonizingly long and tedious, heated or hilarious—and were usually some

Group meeting: *Seated on ground, left to right,* Bill McLarney, Marsha Johnson, Earle Barnhart (on the tire), Susan Ervin (skeining wool), and Don Estes; *at head of table,* Tyrone Cashman; *at far side of table,* Nancy Todd, Susannah Todd, and Bryce Butler; *on near side of table,* Hilde Maingay and John Todd.

The gardens at the New Alchemy Institute in the mid-1970s.

combination of all these. Domestic chores and upkeep of the house and grounds were shared by everyone under the rotating leadership of an "ogre of the week."

It was over this first year on the Farm that we evolved our explanation of New Alchemy's mission as a search for alternative and sustainable ways to provide basic human needs, focusing initially on food, energy, and shelter. Each of these needs, in our view, was complex, multifaceted, and linked conceptually and physically with the others. As we had at the ranch in California, we were looking to the natural world for the clues to develop a science and supporting technologies in its image, mimicking its materials, processes, and dynamics. Such a science would draw on renewable resources. There could be no pollution. We would find ways to recycle wastes.

Amid all this activity, a sense of group identity was beginning to coalesce. After our first summer I wrote: "The world turned copper. The leaves fell. Summer of seventy-two fades into the past. And yet, so much that was fantasy, plan, or theory as the summer began has edged into the realm of reality. We have planted and harvested our first gardens and the data from them are being processed. Many people have come and gone, leaving something of themselves and giving us a sense of being part of a force larger than ourselves that is growing and is very real. The summer is gone; yet we have feasted and laughed and dreamed together. We have learned to love one another. We have begun."

chapter two

Food from Our Gardens and Our Trees

It seems to me that our three basic needs, for food and security and love, are so mixed and mingled and entwined that we cannot straightly think of one without the others. So it happens that when I write of hunger, I am really writing about love and the hunger for it, and warmth and the love of it. . . . And then the warmth and richness and fine reality of hunger satisfied . . . and it is all one.

—M.F.K. Fisher

During the spring preceding New Alchemy's move to the Farm, John and I were contacted by a British journalist serving with the United Nations Educational, Scientific, and Cultural Organization (UNESCO) in Paris who had gotten wind of what we were doing. He invited us to attend a UNESCO conference that was to serve as a warm-up for the famous Stockholm United Nations Environmental Conference later that same year. In late April 1972, John and I and our children boarded a transatlantic flight for our first round of meetings in the international arena. To our surprise we found ourselves being treated as equal players in a growing international movement. The discussions that we had begun years earlier in our living room had become the subject matter of United Nations debate.

It was at UNESCO that we were first exposed to what has since come to be known as the north/south dichotomy. We listened to delegates from Brazil, Indonesia, and other countries describe conditions of poverty and desperation that, to them, made our worries about the environment seem superficial. The ensuing discussions made it painfully clear that our lack of both data and compelling models for sustainable infrastructures was the most serious obstacle in convincing others of the workability of our ideas. Substantiated critique of the existing industrial paradigm was inadequate. No one was going to be converted by our theories. Alternatives had to be rendered visible and proved workable. Another Aha! moment. It was then John and I fully realized how essential it was for New Alchemy to concentrate on a practical nuts-and-bolts focus—to be a place that convinced people that we could live both sustainably and well.

As we had decided to focus New Alchemy's research on sustainable practices for providing basic human needs, it followed logically that we would devote a large part of our attention toward growing food. At that time organic agriculture was not nearly as widespread as it is now; it had yet to prove itself in the public mind. When we began our own research, most of us had gleaned some experience in gardening during our homesteading phase, but none of us qualified as an expert. Undaunted, by the time we had signed the lease for the Farm in November 1971, we were ready to get started on a larger scale. We spent the rest of that fall and the following winter clearing brush from a lower pasture to prepare for gardens the following spring.

As planting time grew near, Rich and Yedida Merrill arrived from California with their kids and set up residence in a tent behind the farmhouse. Their knowledge and experience were fundamental to the unfolding of New Alchemy's gardening program. Hilde Maingay worked closely with them. As we were getting under way, Rich ran soil tests in the former pasture we had designated for growing food. The tests indicated an urgent need for organic matter—lots of it! Rich called for remedial measures. Responding to the challenge, we peeled away from the Farm in our battered pickup and any other vehicles we could commandeer, advancing upon supermarkets and school and hospital cafeterias to make off with any food remains they were willing to let us have. Back at the Farm we combined our hauls with seaweed (mainly eelgrass), grass cuttings, cranberry leaves, and composted horse (or any other animal) manure we could come up with. Over that summer we accumulated enough organic material to make almost 20 tons of compost, which we aged in long windrows before gradually digging it into the garden as we found the time. This was the first step in the ongoing nurturing of the soil until over the years we had transformed it from glacial till into fertile loam—in its own way a visible form of alchemy.

More immediately satisfying at that time was the food we were growing for our own consumption. As the summer went on, we harvested as much as or more than we could eat of tomatoes, cucumbers, zucchinis, pumpkins, and assorted squashes. We also had good yields of beans, lima beans, corn, carrots, turnips, and beets. Many of us were excited to grow peppers and eggplants successfully for the first time. Our only real disappointment was the lettuce crop, which got off to a late start, grew slowly, and was quite bitter. Nonetheless, we had proved that unpromising soil could be nurtured to yield generously. Equally important, we had learned that, with a little guidance, inexperienced gardeners could grow organic foods and eat abundantly and well from the fruit of their own labors.

We conducted our first study that could more conventionally qualify as research in conjunction with Robert Rodale, a leader in the restorative agriculture movement. Through the Rodale Press and its *Organic Gardening and Farming* (*OGF*) magazine, we had organized a Readers Research program with several hundred people conducting experiments in their home gardens. The plan was to have investigators look at natural insect resistance in leafy vegetables. We intended to compile data based on plant variety, soil, and climatic conditions. Unfortunately, before we got very far, although the Readers Research program had attracted several hundred would-be amateur scientists, the Rodale Press had to undergo a period of fiscal belt tightening and after the first summer withdrew its sponsorship. From then on, with a few exceptions, all our experimental work took place at the Farm.

In our own gardens Hilde Maingay conducted a study called the Companion Planting and Insect Resistance Program, through which we sought to replicate the experiments of the *OGF* readers. Because of the sensitivity of cabbages to insect pests, she selected ten varieties for testing. That first summer the susceptible cabbages attracted three major waves of insects: aphids led off, followed by flea beetles, with the annihilating blow being delivered by the larvae of the deceptively pretty cabbage butterfly. It was a hard lesson in the level of skills and knowledge it takes to grow food organically, but this led to the integration of companion planting with herbs and flowers the next year with much improved results. Hilde's data, along with those of participating readers, were compiled after harvest and subsequently reported by Rich in *Organic Gardening and Farming*. "New models for a land-based agriculture are not apt to come from organized science," he predicted, "but from the ability of local groups to use their own kind of inquiry." This proved not only the first but the last report of its kind.

To our disappointment Rich and Yedida could not join us in subsequent years, but we had learned so much from them and were confident that we could manage on our own. In February of the second year on the Farm, Hilde, armed with a variety of gardening manuals and innumerable seed catalogs, sat down to begin planning the gardens. As a guideline, we had agreed on the goal of a garden that would provide vegetables for twenty people for a year. The first outcome of Hilde's efforts was a giant chart that ran the length of the kitchen wall. With accompanying maps of the garden, it was designed so that anyone, visitors included, who wanted to help with the planting could check the chart under the appropriate

The Experimental Cabbage Patch, with Hilde Maingay, her son Sven, and Dave Engstrom.

date, find the list of seeds to be planted, and locate on the map the plot and the row in which to plant them. Dealing as we did with large numbers of people stopping by and wanting to help, it made it possible for them to understand, with minimal explanation, what they could do and how to set about it.

Over the years, under Hilde's direction, the gardens kept getting progressively better. One summer we framed the plots with marigold seedlings that grew to be hedges. Although marigolds are alleged to be an insect repellent, we found they served more as trap plants or decoys that attracted pests away from other crops. At times during July, there seemed to be a Japanese beetle for every marigold blossom, but the gardens were almost completely free of aphids. We were learning that in a garden where diversity is considered fundamental, the agricultural ecosystem can harbor a symbiotic insect population. In addition to bountiful crops of vegetables, one year we grew a magnificent field of sunflowers that eventually stretched to 14 feet in height. By August we had a sunflower jungle, green and shaded, where one could lose oneself on the sunniest days. The seeds were used to feed people, chickens, and the rabbits that Hilde had added to our internal food cycle. The chickens and rabbits contributed manure to the compost and eventually became the main dish for group dinners. We also had a successful crop of soybeans, which we not only cooked in various ways to feed ourselves but also ground to feed the fish.

John Todd and a Saturday visitor turning the compost.

After several seasons of concentrating on intensive growing techniques and high productivity, Hilde introduced raised beds and sheet composting to our garden management. From French intensive methods she adapted the close spacing of plants in order to reduce weeds and retain water. "This type of horticulture," she reported, "also uses mulching and composting, techniques that have been established over thousands of years, in conjunction with the new understanding and knowledge gleaned from modern science. . . . It uses simple, low-cost equipment, does not rely on nonrenewable fossil fuels for fertilizers and pesticides, and uses the soil area and the sun's energy effectively. Over time the soil is improved and the production and quality of the crop is increased, while labor and materials from the outside remains stable or declines."

Hilde found the raised beds more convenient to work and maintain than those at ground level. In a garden as large and occasionally overpopulated as ours, a clear distinction between walkways and growing areas was a distinct advantage. The beds were rotated seasonally. Trench or sheet composting involved spreading thin layers of organic materials such as grass clippings, dry leaves, seaweed, garden wastes, and occasionally straw in the pathways. This helped maintain the shape of the beds, kept them from overheating and drying out, and prevented the sidewalls from collapsing. We took great pride in the exotic range of manures we were able to add as composted fertilizer. Once or twice after the County Fair we brought back not only goat but tiger and elephant leavings, which, we felt, added to the distinction of our gardening practices.

We buried all the organic materials accumulated along with those in the pathways beneath a layer of topsoil at the end of the season. The new techniques were extremely effective in controlling or almost eliminating weeds, in reducing the need for watering, and in helping to cope with insect pests. We had little significant damage from whiteflies, aphids, or flea beetles. We picked cabbage worms and squash borers off by hand and were able to keep them under control. Cucumber and Mexican bean beetles, however, remained major foes and almost devastated their designated crops until we started to experiment with integrated pest management (IPM). As much as we dreaded the pests, we happily welcomed and nurtured the allies that chose to appear, such as ladybird beetles, praying mantis, toads, and birds whose dietary preferences helped us hold our own and maintain the balance of the garden.

Since the prodigious drive of the first summer, we had not assigned anyone to oversee our ongoing composting efforts. Several years later, this task fell to new volunteer Ty Cashman. Temporarily setting aside his recent PhD in philosophy, Ty gamely set to work and before long was turning out about 8 tons of compost every four weeks. After his first few weeks on the job, our new *chef de compost* allowed that he had learned his first lesson in stewardship. "In writing you do the work," he announced. "In composting nature does the work." It was the first year that we had someone specifically overseeing the compost pile, ensuring that it was properly fed and brewing at all times. The results were soon markedly visible. A number of us, when giving a tour of the garden, adopted the tactic of gesturing toward a pile of dirt, consisting largely of sand that had been dug up for some project, and explaining that this had been typical of the whole garden prior to compost. It succeeded in drawing attention to what was becoming dark, fecund soil. Like us, people were generally favorably impressed with the applied alchemy of composting.

As our last killing frost on the Cape can occur as late as mid-May and return by mid-September, Hilde decided to experiment with various means of extending the growing season. Her most successful technique was based on a modification of the traditional bell-shaped glass cloche that originated in France in the nineteenth century. A cloche was placed over a plant, in the manner of a tea cozy over a teapot, to protect it from frost damage and force growth. As one cloche per plant in a garden the size of ours was ludicrous, Hilde reinvented it to suit her purposes. The resulting Quonset-like plant covers consisted of curved sections of translucent sheeting attached to rectangular wooden frames with doors at either end. They ran the length and width of a raised bed and, in size and appearance, were

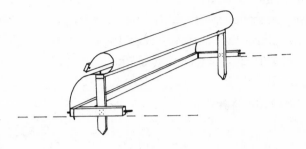

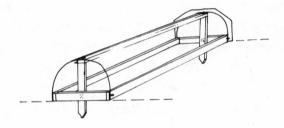

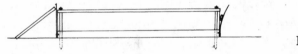

Hilde's cloche.

a hybrid of cloche and a small greenhouse. "The difference in growth was strik-ing," Hilde reported. "A month after setting out, the plants under the extended cloche were two to three times as big as the controls. Two months after the plant-ing date we harvested the first broccoli. The plants kept producing until the sec-ond week of October. Eggplants, tomatoes, and Bibb lettuce as well as basil also matured a month earlier. We were still picking vegetables in mid-November."

As productivity continued to improve over the seasons, Hilde summarized her results as follows: "On one plot of less than an acre we grew one serving each of a raw vegetable, a green cooked vegetable, and a root or other nongreen cooked vegetable for ten people for every day of the year with some surplus." Such abun-dance led her to postulate: "Gardening intensively on a small acreage, using such practices as extending the season with cloches and solar-heated greenhouses, se-lecting local plant varieties for pest and disease resistance and for suitability to soil and climate, improving soil fertility, establishing food-producing forests, and

animal husbandry are all strategies within our reach to heal the Earth and to secure the existence of future generations. All that is needed is people willing to
tend the land and nurture the plants that in turn sustain them."

Because Hilde was pleased with our increasingly abundant harvests, she became interested in local agricultural history and decided to do a bit of research.
Curious to know whether she might expect such bounty regularly, she called the
local agricultural extension agent to ask about average yields of vegetables and
grains on Cape Cod. "I'm sorry," the agent told her, "but I can't give you any such
data. The Cape cannot produce anything but cranberries and some strawberries."
Hilde tried again. "Maybe you have records on crops grown here twenty years or
so ago." His reply was again negative; he had not seen anything else growing successfully in the twenty years he had been on the job. Hilde persisted. "What about
a *long* time ago, the turn of the century or before?" Another negative answer:
"Lady, you don't want to know about those figures because what they called high
yields back then, we call a poor yield now." Hilde noted, "If I hadn't already grown
an abundance of vegetables on our land, I should have stopped gardening and
gone into the construction business." Yet once again, by the end of that season,
the garden had surpassed its previous record. Hilde and her crew had grown more
food with less work and less irrigation than the previous year. She did not record
whether she checked back in with the extension agent.

By the late 1970s, New Alchemy's organic yields were consistently three times
greater than the Department of Agriculture's estimates for average yields for a
comparable acreage using agricultural fertilizers, herbicides, and pesticides. A
major factor in this success was persistent attention to soil improvement. In addition to the other measures to achieve this, Hilde at one point had a brain wave
that ensured us a virtually inexhaustible supply of organic matter. On our frequent trips to the "Falmouth Disposal Area," we saw that there was an autumnal
harvest of leaves raked from area lawns for the taking. A few hand-made signs
redirecting leaf-bearing cars and trucks to the Farm soon brought vast deposits of
leaves, which we stacked in long windrows at the upper end of the gardens. The
people dropping off the leaves seemed glad to do so, and we received all we could
use. As we later came to say, waste is just a resource out of place. The soil responded by growing ever more fertile. We used the leaves for winter mulches and
for sheet or trench composting between the raised beds.

One summer, wanting to explore further the potential for regional food self-
sufficiency on Cape Cod, we undertook our most ambitious agricultural experiment to date and decided to grow wheat. We had been told that the Cape had once
been the breadbasket of the Boston area, but that wheat had not been grown locally for a hundred years. Undaunted, we were determined to try, although find-

Nancy Todd harvesting wheat.

ing seed in our area became our first obstacle and a task that cost Bob Angevine endless phone calls, letters, and arguments. When he finally acquired it, we planted in late May. There were no problems with germination, and during succeeding weeks the wheat grew well, holding its own in spite of competition from the weeds. By late July we had achieved a fine field of waving wheat, the tops of which just exceeded the waving weeds. We chose to consider this not too bad an effort for a first try. At least, we now knew that we could grow wheat on Cape Cod. Then we were faced with the problem of harvesting it. After much pondering we settled on the plan of waiting till Saturday, when there would be more help, and picking it by hand.

Saturday arrived and harvesting began. The first hour was great fun. We would gather up great armloads of stalks and totter to the edge of the field bearing enormous sheaves. By the second hour we were beginning to wonder why the picked section had grown so little in relation to the vast area that remained to be cleared. By the third hour conversations had begun to lag and the crowd had thinned perceptibly. By the end of a long dusty day we had managed to pick no more than a ragged little patch in what by then seemed a great expanse of wheat field. We were definitely discouraged.

Monday came and Bob Angevine managed to track down an ancient cutter. Escaping the office, he mounted it and moved through the field, mowing down wheat and weeds alike in no time. The next step lay in separating the wheat from the weeds. This we did by passing it through a shredder-grinder with the bottom plates replaced by bars. After that, there remained winnowing the wheat from the chaff—literally. At first Earle Barnhart tried using a vacuum cleaner to force air upward through a large tube and blow off the chaff. It worked, but when he found that the wheat could be only collected a cup at a time, he fell back on the traditional method of winnowing, tossing it in the air and letting the chaff drift off on the wind.

The project cost us a great deal of time, but overall we did not begrudge it. In a perverse way we had enjoyed our adventure. It gave us confidence that, if necessary, wheat could be grown in what would be considered an inhospitable area and that problems of harvesting and processing on a small-scale or homesteading basis were not insurmountable. And in growing a grain that is considered a staff of life we found an underlying, almost joyous feeling, which perhaps could be attributed partly to working in a field of ripe wheat, and partly to the half-conscious realization that in harvesting and storing for the coming winter, we were re-enacting a timeless ritual that linked us to generations long before and hopefully long after us.

As the regular gardens evolved and grew more diverse, we noticed changes in the insect populations. Some years the cabbage butterfly, which had so devastated some of Hilde's early crops, largely passed us by. Others, like the squash borer, sometimes attacked with persistence and left us with the novel experience of too few zucchini. The Mexican bean beetle was a scourge of the garden for several years. Dried beans being an inexpensive and nutritious source of protein, Susan Ervin, who was another of the leaders in the gardening research, was interested in testing as many varieties as possible; but although we would spend days and days picking bright yellow larvae off the bean plants by hand, they came on again and again in waves, like the barbarian invaders of the Roman Empire. They decimated the lima beans and made pathetic, derelict stumps of the kidney beans; and although we salvaged a few green beans, they were a mere handful in relation to the number of plants. Such labor-intensive pest control in terms of work hours was backbreaking for us and, we realized, completely impractical for a commercial grower. Like all warfare, however, our battle with the Mexican bean beetle led to an escalation in our defenses, and the following year, at Susan's initiative, we launched our first program in integrated pest management.

Susan reported on our early experiment in an article in one of our newsletters entitled "Mexican Bean Battles." "We are prepared to accept some insect damage; the disappointment of a low yield from one crop is usually balanced by a good yield from another," she explained. "But, year after year, severe bean beetle—*Epilachna varivestis*—infestations have reduced plants to skeletons." Researching the problem drew her attention to experiments in which a gnat-sized predatory wasp from India, *Pediobius faveolatus,* had been used as a biological control agent for the bean beetle. The wasps deposit their eggs inside the larvae of the beetles, which then turn brown and die. The next generation of wasps hatches out of these "mummies" in twelve to twenty-six days. *Pediobius faveolatus,* she further learned, were host-specific and would not parasitize other insects. Susan sent for a batch of wasps and our first experiment in IPM was under way. Although we still incurred some bean beetle damage, we saw enough parasitization to know we had a potential solution within reach. As Susan learned more about appropriate numbers, timing of release, and placement of the larval wasps, she was able to produce good yields of many varieties of beans.

With succeeding growing seasons we came to take the bounty of the gardens pretty much for granted. Although Hilde and Susan continued to experiment with variables, testing mulches and watering techniques, and expanding the IPM program, by the late 1970s the basic regimen for the garden was well established. As the size of the group expanded, the productivity of the garden responded accordingly. We still grew all the vegetables we could use, as well as fruits such as melons and strawberries. By the time regular testing showed the soil lacking in none of the essential nutrients, Hilde could well afford to laugh at the memory of the glacial till she had first tried to coax food from. She now had her statistics on productivity at the quick: On one-tenth of an acre in the intensive beds, she was able to grow three portions of vegetables for thirteen adults year-round. At that time, the national farm average required three times as much land for the same output.

One year, our artist in residence, Jeff Parkin, who worked mainly with Bill in aquaculture, became involved in raising earthworms. He did so not only because worms made excellent and protein-laden meals for fish, but also because of their role in enhancing soil fertility. In those energy-conscious days of the early 1970s, we were also interested in what we called their energetically efficient recycling capabilities as bioconverters. In his report "Some Other Friends of the Earth," Jeff explained, "As we become compelled to orient our solutions for the wastefulness of society towards longer-term stability, we should do well to include the earthworm. If nothing (and optimistically more than anything else), I hope this brings an appreciation of what lies beneath our feet."

What could not have been gleaned about our gardens from the various reports was their beauty and their role in bonding us to the land and to each other. If New Alchemy could have been said to have a soul, it was unquestionably the garden, where our food was grown and where so many of us spent time working together, occasionally silent but more often talking. And as time passed, it was just as well

The garden in the mid-1970s.

that we had learned so much about agriculture. The early 1980s and the economic policies of the Reagan administration brought a drastic shortfall in foundation support, challenging the gardens—and the gardeners—on a new front. It was the economic bottom line that was to drive all New Alchemy programs, including agriculture, from then on.

Our research gained new dimensions. We needed to investigate existing organic market gardens in order to establish major production costs and see how economic performance could be improved using more extensive composting, green manures, biological pest control, and biological herbicides. The objective was to evolve strategies that might result in better returns for the farmer. By the early 1980s we could no longer be solely engaged in research; we also had to be competitive in terms of the market. Our head gardeners of that era, Steve Tracy and, later, Dave Marchant, rose to the challenge. The dreaded bottom line drove the agriculture program to unforeseen levels of productivity, which was accomplished without depleting the soil. Steve sold his produce to restaurants and

Hilde Maingay (left) and Susan Ervin chopping cabbage for coleslaw.

health food stores and at local growers' markets, bringing in an unprecedented $4,000 in gross revenues in his first year. Building on Steve's precedent, David Marchant eventually netted a whopping $10,000 from garden produce. In spite of added pressure from the so-called real world, we were annually demonstrating that informed stewardship could achieve sustainably, organically, and at low cost the high yields that agribusiness, the green revolution, and today's genetic engineering seek at unknown economic and environmental risks.

A Farm in the Image of the Forest

By the late 1970s New Alchemy's agricultural innovation was also moving in a new direction. Because Earle Barnhart was concerned with eroding ecosystems, he was turning his attention to what he then called a permanent agricultural landscape. Planning to establish an arboretum of locally adapted fruit and nut trees on the Farm, he began an extensive tree-planting program. His eventual goal was to create a mixed and sustainable agricultural landscape. We found his expanding population of young trees satisfying not only because it embodied an ecological ethic, but because it was a gesture that invested in rather than robbed the future.

In one of our publications, Earle explained, "At New Alchemy we are interested in reintegrating existing knowledge of traditional farming methods with fundamental ecological principles. The need is to generate new agricultures that would mirror the workings of nature, using renewable energy and appropriate technology to insure reasonable productivity and environmental permanence. The general limits of the ecosystem would be determined biogeographically, simulating naturally occurring climatic climax communities. The agricultural landscape for an American eastern forest biogeographic province would be different to that of the central plains region. The biotic components would include climatically adapted, multiple-use plants and animals, both wild and domestic."

Earle was soon joined by swashbuckling New Zealander and fellow tree enthusiast John Quinney. Under their leadership, New Alchemy's agricultural forestry program drew new people like a magnet. The number of tree people, as they called themselves, quickly expanded to half a dozen or so. The tree team also included some important nonhuman members—a small flock of Chinese weeding geese whose assignment was to graze the grass pasture beneath the fruit, nut, and fodder tress. John Quinney wrote of the geese: "In their own unique and often lovable manner these creatures have impressed us. As biological lawnmowers, fertilizer spreaders, and herbicides they are effective replacements for machinery and fossil fuels."

John was interested in the potential economics of what we were calling forest farming in New England. "If the dual concerns of maintaining ecological integrity and making a profit from farming small acreages can be satisfied," he explained, "we will have assembled a powerful demonstration of the agricultural potential on Cape Cod with applications throughout southern New England." With the three-dimensional space of the forest as the design model, John and the tree people drew up a set of guidelines to establish procedures. The first of these was to look to the process of succession as a creator of pattern. John saw this as a dynamic process, beginning at the bottom of the fishponds and extending up to the vegetable and forage crop zones, then to the shrub layer and the canopy formed by the trees that produced fruit, nut, timber, and fodder crops. In this way a sustainably productive landscape with great potential for food production could evolve over the years. The polar opposite of monoculture landscapes, this three-dimensional, time-lapse approach imitates a maturing natural system in diversity and multifunctionality. The ponds would be used to grow fish and provide irrigation water for vegetable, grain, and forage crops for human and animal consumption. The forested areas, while also productive, provide protection in the form of windbreaks, the prevention of leaching, erosion control, and habitat for birds to aid in insect control.

The tree people, minus the geese, also established a small perennial ecological island to provide a stable supply of pollen for Earle Barnhart's bees. In the lee of an evergreen windbreak, they planted pussywillows and more than fifty kinds of herbs and flowers. The tree people were additionally propagating and testing persimmon, kiwi, jujube, blueberries, elderberries, catalpa, buckeyes, Korean pine nut, and shagbark hickory. In doing so they were bringing to bear the same nurturing policies that had characterized the rejuvenation of the soil in the garden from worn-out pasture to its later productive state.

John Quinney also worked with nitrogen-fixing trees and shrubs. "In the agricultural forestry work at New Alchemy," he noted, "nitrogen-fixing trees and shrubs are important components of the overall ecology." The tree people began with a collection of honey locust, black locust, Scotch broom, autumn olive, and bayberry. They were testing these tree crops as hedgerows, windscreens, and living fences, as habitat for birds and other insect predators, for biological pest control, and as a source of structural materials. With more experience they reduced their use of nonnative species and concentrated on indigenous trees and shrubs. They also established hedgerows and mixed stands of trees, intending that, according to John, "careful integration of a variety of nitrogen-fixing species in our agricultural forests will make a substantial contribution to the productivity of the forests in a way that is both energetically and environmentally gentle."

A farm in the image of the forest was also intended to serve as an umbrella concept for a model farm for New England. By the early 1980s, in spite of record productivity, it was generally felt that we had not as yet achieved a full synthesis in our agriculture program. John Todd and John Quinney maintained, "Our Cape Cod center is currently a patchwork of separate projects in aquaculture, field crops, soil and pest management, bioshelter research, perennial crops, new feedstock experiments, poultry, pasture management ideas, and tree crops evaluation. Until all these programs were tested and proved valid on their own, it was not possible to create a synthesis. Over the past decade we have found a positive answer to our original question as to whether ecology could be used as the basis for design in agriculture, energy and architecture. We are now at the point of asking if an ecological synthesis will result in a new and sound economic base for agriculture, particularly on small acreages in New England. New Alchemy is going to attempt to create a 'science of assembly' into which the best intellectual ingredients, both traditional and modern, are put together in new forms." This program remained central to New Alchemy throughout the life of the Institute.

chapter three

Food from Our Fishponds

Give a man a fish and you feed him for a day.
Teach a man to fish and you feed him for a lifetime.
—Old Chinese Proverb

Gratified as we were to be proving the viability of our organic horticultural methods, we were also determined to learn to produce substantial amounts of protein. Many of us had traveled in countries such as India, Haiti, and Indonesia and returned haunted by memories of weak, underfed children and painfully thin adults. Aware then—and all the more so now—of malnutrition in many more places in the world, we reasoned that if we could devise methods of growing fish that interested local people and were also inexpensive and ecologically sustainable, it could offer them a measure of independence as well as reliable nutrition.

It must also be admitted that Bill McLarney was born fascinated with fish. His passion cannot be understated. He accurately has been called both a fish freak and a fish maniac. Fortunately, there was a time-honored tradition that justified Bill's enthusiasm, and his launching of the aquaculture season was another dominant dynamic of our first summer on the Farm. As he had pointed out in an article in *American Fish Farmer*, "American fish culturists would do well to study the example of Chinese and Southeast Asia fish farmers, who habitually exceed our best yields without the benefit of our technology." As he had pointed out, over thousands of years Asian peoples, particularly the Chinese, had developed methods of producing high yields of fish with low inputs of money and technology. Chinese fish culturists, as

Bill knew, took advantage of a pond environment by stocking several types of fish to achieve what is called a polyculture. They further enhanced productivity by integrating the pond with terrestrial farming, using vegetable wastes as fish food and manures as pond fertilizers. Wastes and enriched water from the pond were applied in turn to the land. In tropical parts of Asia, combining Chinese techniques with a year-round growing season produced record yields. This was the model for Bill's aquaculture program both on the Cape and in Costa Rica.

As Bill and his coauthors noted in their 1973 book, *Aquaculture*, their success could be attributed to their recognition of two facts:

1. A body of water is a three-dimensional growing space. To treat it like a field, by planting only one kind of crop, is likely to result in wasting the majority of that space.
2. Any fertile pond will produce a number of different fish food organisms. However, most fish are not omnivorous, but rather selective in their diet. Thus stocking single species wastes not only space but food.

Although polyculture on the Southeast Asia model was our eventual goal, the fish on which we first chose to concentrate for intensive culture was tilapia. Tilapia has been an important food fish in Africa, the Near East, and Southeast Asia for thousands of years. They appear on a number of art objects from the Egypt of the pharaohs. Tilapia is sometimes called Saint Peter's fish; legend holds that tilapia was the fish with which Christ miraculously fed the multitudes. Almost unknown as a food fish in North America until Bill began his research, tilapia are now widely available here. Intrigued as he was by their ancient pedigree, however, Bill was more interested in the fact that tilapia are largely herbivorous, easy to breed, hardy, and have a good flavor. Among the twenty possible species of tilapia used in fish culture, he settled on *Tilapia aurea* (now renamed *Sarotherodon aurea*), which mainly feed on planktonic algae, and *Tilapia zillii*, which favor vegetables. We had worked with them in the dome pond at our house for the Readers Research program and had harvested more than four hundred young fish, which we held indoors over the winter for the next growing season. It seemed worthwhile to continue with them.

During our first summer at the Farm we dug nine circular ponds 16 feet in diameter and about 3 feet deep. We covered two of them with double-skinned, translucent domes to serve as season extenders. We used 6-millimeter polyethylene sheets to line the sides of the ponds. The only difference between the two covered ponds was that one incorporated a recirculating water filter system. The rationale behind this was that fish tend to emit growth-inhibiting metabolites at high population densities. We could have corrected the situation by enlarging the

Tilapia aurea.

pond or thinning the population, but we found that for our purposes it was more practical to remove the growth-inhibiting compounds with a bacterial filter analogous to the sand filters used by aquarium hobbyists. With this type of filter, water was pumped up from the pond and through a bed of oyster shells or other calcareous material, then back into the pond. The shells served as both physical and chemical buffers, removing particulate matter and buffering pH. Their principal function was as a substrate for the bacteria that broke down the growth-inhibiting substances.

Algae—aquatic plant matter—were the basis of the diet of the tilapia. To maintain algal growth in the ponds, we inserted large pieces of hard clamshell (quahog, pronounced "co-hog" by Cape locals) into our filters. The density of the algae was measured periodically with a Secchi disc, which consists of a metal plate painted in alternating sectors of black and white and suspended on a measured string. When the disc was visible below 2 feet, indicating an inadequate algae supply, Bill took one or both of two corrective measures to restore algal density: he would either remove about 10 percent of the pond volume and replace it with freshwater, or add a small amount of horse manure "tea," which was kept inside the dome in a retired refrigerator liner.

From the start the tilapia grew, thrived, and reproduced, and our first fish crop was deemed a success. At the end of the season another healthy and growing population had been established, and we were able to keep the fish alive over the winter, although they grew very little. When spring arrived, they were in good health and ready to jump-start the new year's program. Bill's proudest achievement his first year was that he managed to avoid using commercial fish foods. He

Bill McLarney in the
dome with aquaculture
pond.

felt that this was important not only because commercial feeds can be expensive
and draw on ingredients that can feed people directly, but because they are rarely
available or affordable to growers most in need of a cheap, reliable food source.
So, to supplement the algae diet of the tilapia, he experimented with a number of
plant and animal foods. As he noted in a subsequent newsletter: "A large variety
of greens have been offered to our fish with varying results. The two most readily accepted are purslane and carrot tops." Ground soybeans, he found, also met
with favor. Because the young of even the most exemplary of vegetarians among
fish require some animal protein, Bill also slipped them such gourmet fare as
earthworms and insects.

Another year Bill and John Todd, out of either scientific curiosity or a desire to
bring an element of excitement to the daily rounds of caring for the fish, chose a
two-pronged strategy. One lot of fish was housed as usual in a dome pond and
was the charge of Bill's team; John's team covered another pond with clear plastic glazing to create a low, flat-topped structure they dubbed the Alter Ego. Each
team had its own opinion on the best fish diets, and they compared notes like

Early bioshelter—the Alter Ego—with windmill and subsurface fishponds.

young mothers vying to see whose baby would be the first to accept solid foods. John favored plants and algae with a protein supplement in the form of zooplankton or microscopic aquatic animals. Bill provided more varied fare with supplemental soy and insect larvae. At the final harvesting and weigh-in the total weights were very close. Both sides were a bit deflated that they could not claim to have proved the superiority of their methods, but they had managed to grow tilapia to edible size in just ten weeks.

Our confidence in the aquaculture program was challenged one August Saturday in 1974 with the arrival of the food editor of the *New York Times,* John Hess and his wife, Karen. They toured the Farm and proved extraordinarily sympathetic to what we were doing. As they were about to leave, John Hess flung down his gauntlet: "Granted, growing inexpensive, high-quality protein is useful, even necessary. But how do your tilapia taste?"

We were taken aback. We thought the fish delicious, but we were experimenting in protein production, not in raising a product to meet the exacting standards of a well-known food critic. Our opinion did not satisfy Mr. Hess, who allowed that he would like to find out for himself. He asked if they could come back for a taste trial, volunteering Karen to do the cooking. Nervously, we agreed on the following Tuesday. Armed with nets and fishing lines, Bill and John with most of the kids set out that morning to garner the catch. To our delight, a rather neglected

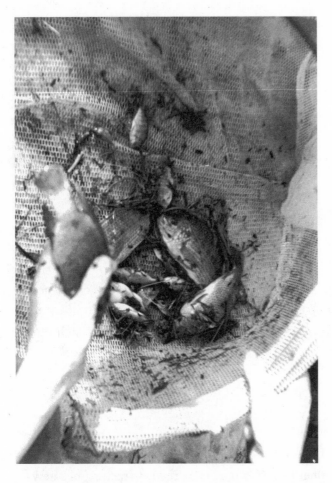

Weighing young tilapia.

pond netted fourteen plump tilapia, many weighing over half a pound. Bill, assisted by an enthusiastic if unskilled staff of small boys, was in charge of the cleaning. Mrs. Hess, a superb and experienced cook, then took over. Rejecting more exotic recipes, she fried some of the tilapia and baked others in foil. She used only salt, pepper, lemon, and parsley for seasoning.

When the fish were ready, we bore the tilapia-laden platters out to the picnic table where the rest of the meal had already been arranged. We all clustered about, anxiously trying to read the facial expressions of the Hesses as they sampled. Cautious tasting sounds ensued. After a few moments of concentration they announced, with unqualified enthusiasm, that the tilapia had far exceeded their expectations. They were, they maintained, unquestionably superior to any hatchery-raised fish they had ever tried.

We were nonetheless still a bit apprehensive. We had been following John Hess's columns as he toured local restaurants, which he found lackluster at best. Aware of his high standards, we awaited public judgment on our tilapia. A week or so later the *New York Times* arrived. We crowded around, hastily rifling through

Serving-size tilapia weighing about half a pound each.

the pages and scanning over one another's shoulders. We found the heading: "Farm Raised Fish: A Triumph for the Sensualist and the Ecologist." It was far better than we had dared hope. Our tilapia had achieved a successful, high-profile debut and had been pronounced a triumph by no less than the *New York Times*.

Fish in Cages

Once Bill had his ponds at the Farm producing reliably, he and his assistant and New Alchemy's artist in residence, Jeff Parkin, were ready to tack off in a new direction in his aquaculture research. His plan was to grow fish in floating cages in the natural environment. There was a shallow pond well suited to his purpose on the northwest border of the Farm. "The implication of successful fish culture in cages," he explained, "is that anyone with access to unpolluted standing water could raise fish for the table and perhaps for sale. The fish are confined in a small space, which simplifies feeding, inspection, and harvesting." As with our other systems, the idea was to produce fish at a low cost and in quantities appropriate for homestead use. By dint of using a small space but not a small volume of water, cage culture did not require the recirculation and filtration systems that most of our other arrangements did.

"Cage culture has the further advantage," Bill wrote, "of being one of the few methods of fish culture that is compatible with the other values and uses of a pond. A pond like Grassy Pond, with its extensive shallows, brush and weeds, irregular shore line, and natural fish predators, viewed solely from food fish production standpoint, is very inefficient. But to convert it to a conventionally effi-

One of the fish cages on the pond.

cient fish culture pond would seriously compromise or destroy its value in terms of sport fishing and other recreational use, wildlife habitat, and aesthetic pleasure. To use it for cage culture modifies only a few square feet of the pond's surface. The cages may even enhance fishing; we find that bullheads, in particular, tend to congregate under the cages, fattening on morsels which slip by the caged fish."

Bill built three 64-cubic-foot mesh cages that had rigid wooden frames around the upper rim but were otherwise unsupported. Flotation was provided by strips of Styrofoam attached near the top so that a quarter of the 4-foot-high cages rose above the surface of the water. The Styrofoam was enclosed in canvas bags to prevent it from breaking up and floating loose in the pond. Nylon line anchored the cages to cinder blocks on the pond bottom.

As with his other efforts in fish raising, Bill was anxious about overreliance on commercial feeds. "There are numerous manufacturers of dry feeds for trout and catfish," he told New Alchemy followers. "Scientifically inclined readers may be appalled at the energetics of formulating such a feed. Others will question the appropriateness of feeding fish on potentially useful human food. Still others will criticize the ethics or politics of using inexpensive fish from the coasts of South America to make expensive fish for the North American table."

Experimenting with raising midge larvae as a source of protein for his fish, Bill came up with some concrete results. (Midges are tiny insects that swarm in warm weather.) The program was carried out under the auspices of the Woods Hole Oceanographic Institution, which Bill acknowledged in his subsequent report in one of our publications. He also slipped in a comment that shed light on attempting to do research outside the unspoken strictures of institutional science: "To offer a blanket acknowledgment of that Institution would be to overlook the massive bureaucratic interference and the attitudes of certain scientists and administrators which nearly prevented our 1974 work from being carried out—a fine example of the sort of frustration which added impetus for some of us to leave 'establishment science' and join forces in New Alchemy."

Obstacles notwithstanding, the focus of his work that year was to further improve on his midge-culturing methods and to test the effectiveness of the larvae as a growth-promoting supplement in fish diets that without commercial feed could otherwise be lacking in protein. Extrapolating from the results at the end of the season, it was estimated that 10 square meters or 12 square yards of substrate could satisfy the supplemental protein requirements of some eighty thousand young fish.

Justified in his hunches, Bill persevered in substituting his own concoctions for commercial feed while Jeff Parkin was kept busy creating blends of alfalfa, comfrey, soy meal, and earthworms, which were dubbed Brand X or Jeff Pie. The fish eventually learned to accept these offerings, but seldom with the enthusiasm that the experimenters would have liked to see. As a mother with nutritional ideas at odds with some of the preferences of my children, I sympathized with Jeff and Bill.

In 1978, after two seasons of disappointing results with the fish cages, Bill and Jeff came in with a bumper crop of bullheads. This time they had hit on the right fish—yellow bullheads. Because of having gotten the season off to a late start, they agreed to compromise and use some commercial feeds. In spite of this, when they calculated their costs, including feeds and construction materials, they found they had produced fish at a per-unit weight of sixty-six cents a pound—a bargain for animal protein. Bill and Jeff encouraged other would-be growers: "The fact is that bullheads are delicious. When we harvested our crop, a portion was fried for the first New Alchemy bullhead feast. Based on the discriminating and satisfied smacking it appears the bullhead has few rivals in texture and taste."

Bill and Jeff's next step was to persist in the search for alternate food sources that could further reduce costs. As they were quick to point out, half of the production budget of the commercial catfish farmer went to feeds. In this research Bill was not running a seat-of-the-pants "maybe they'll eat earthworms, maybe we'll try something else" operation. All his and Jeff's trials were conducted with absolute rigor. Although the results of the trials were mixed, Bill and Jeff concluded that if earthworms were cultivated rather than bought, they made economic sense as a feed supplement and that bullheads particularly would derive significant nutritional benefits. "We feel the most important aspect of our work," they reported, "is to affirm that, at least for the small-scale grower, there are options to dependence on fish-meal based commercial feeds." In proving the applicability of their cage culture methods for raising food fish, Bill and Jeff achieved

Jeff Parkin checking one of the fish cages.

the primary goal of New Alchemy's aquaculture program. They were producing protein not only ecologically but economically with methods that could readily be replicated almost anywhere.

Growing Fish Aboveground

Another of our techniques for intensive fish raising tacked off in a radically new and different direction. It had its start as the sun began to gain strength in the late winter of 1974. One March morning that year John set up three clear 5-gallon glass containers with lids in a tidy row on the grass in front of our house. He filled one, then half-filled the second with tap water. The next day, having given the tap water time to dechlorinate, he trudged down to the seasonal pond below our house and returned with brimming pails. He topped up the second jar to concoct a mixture that was half pond and half tap water. The third he filled entirely with pond water then added what he called "a dense brew of a dark-colored algae cultured from household wastes."

Young tilapia in the
solar-algae tank.

John monitored his contained ecosystems in their jars as spring approached
and the days grew longer. Sun-warmed during the day, two of the three began to
evolve noticeably. While the jar containing only tap water remained clear and un-
changed, the middle jar, which was the mix of tap and pond water grew pale and
then intense green and became less transparent. The third jar with the pond
water and household brew darkened until it was almost black and opaque. John
was pondering whether these jars might be a micromodel or analog of how vegetation regulates climate on a global scale: Might the dense jar be equivalent to a
forest, the intermediate jar to cropped fields, and the clear jar, like the deserts, act
more as a reflector than an absorber? What the children and I were witnessing was
the invention of one of New Alchemy's most singular achievements and, as will
be described in succeeding chapters, the springboard for countless offshoot developments in intensive aquaculture, energy absorption, and water remediation.

The next incarnation of the jars appeared later that summer at the Farm. It took
the form of a column of slender, cylindrical, aquaculture tanks placed in a line
along the edge of a field. The tanks, then being called solar-algae ponds, were 5
feet in height and 18 inches in diameter. They were made of a semitransparent

fiberglass material. We later also worked with larger tanks of the same height, which were 5 feet in circumference and held 734 gallons of water. We experimented with the translucent ponds both indoors and out, working with them in several configurations—singly, coupled in pairs, and linked in longer lines to form what we called a solar river.

The first experiments were to investigate the effects of increasing the area of water surface exposed to sunlight. Not only the upper surface of the water, as in natural systems, but the outer rim of the column was exposed to light through the translucent walls of the tanks. Newcomer and biology graduate from the University of California at Berkeley, Ron Zweig, wrote one of the first reports: "The theory behind experimenting with these ponds is to increase the amount of pond surface area exposed to solar energy. With these tanks, not only is the upper surface exposed to light penetration, as in a traditional pond, [but] light penetrates through the sides of the tank as well. This has proved a most effective means of collecting and storing solar energy."

The tanks, according to Ron, "demonstrated phenomenal productivity" in experiments with high-density fish polyculture. He did a series of trials. One was to determine the maximum population of fish that could be grown per solar-algae pond. He raised them in a brew of what he called "a rich phytoplankton bloom." He found that the smaller ponds, when coupled in pairs, proved the most prolific, but that productivity was excellent in the larger tanks as well. In standard aquaculture, fish productivity is measured in kilograms per hectare. To judge our results, we extrapolated the volume of our tanks and the time span of the growing season to a ratio of hectares per year. The highest record we could find for productivity for pond aquaculture ranged between 1,000 and just over 1,500 kilograms of fish per hectare per year. In its first trial during the summer of 1975, our most prolific solar pond weighed in at more than an extrapolated 140,000 kilograms, a yield almost ten times greater than the best natural pond aquaculture. The second trial yielded encouraging, if not quite so spectacular, results.

By 1978 the high yields of the solar ponds enabled the aquaculture team to obtain a substantial, multiyear grant from the National Science Foundation (NSF). The grant funded the aquaculture research team made up of John Todd, Ron Zweig, Dave Engstrom, and newcomers Al Doolittle and John Wolfe. The goal was to evaluate the solar-algae ponds and to develop ecological models intended to clarify some of their internal dynamics. It was to be a further step in gaining an understanding of whole systems, with the ultimate goal of codifying the conditions that would lead to maximum productivity.

We already knew that the phenomenal productivity of the solar-algae ponds was due to the amount of solar energy entering the pond through the sides of the

Hydroponic lettuces
and cucumbers on top of
solar-algae ponds.

tank. This drove photosynthetic processes that produced large amounts of dissolved oxygen in the water, which increased the primary productivity of the plant life in the pond. This meant we were incubating dense populations of phytoplankton for food for the tilapia. Due to the exposure of the entire column of water to sunlight, water temperatures and oxygen concentrations were more uniform than in a conventional pond. Ron's research with the solar-algae ponds involved working with variables of a monoculture of *Tilapia aurea* and polycultures of tilapia, mirror carp, and grass carp. The results indicated that, in spite of finding high pH, or alkalinity, to be a factor in limiting growth, the solar-algae ponds held up as having extraordinary productivity potential. Ron repeatedly demonstrated that the tilapia grew better in the clear-sided ponds, corroborating a direct link between tilapia growth and phytoplankton photosynthesis. To maximize the productivity of the system, Ron and his team attempted to optimize the tilapia's basic diet of algae with commercial fish feed. Ron had a hunch that the quantity of food was the driving factor in pond productivity. This was vindicated at harvest when he found that by quadrupling the feed he obtained a tenfold increase in fish growth.

The novelty of the solar-algae ponds attracted considerable attention beyond the Farm. According to Ron and John Wolfe, "We continue to be inundated with inquiries about how to raise those funny fish in those whatchamacallit fish tanks." Undistracted, they pushed on with the more technical NSF research with Dave Engstrom. They were studying the water chemistry of the tanks and the interaction of the sunlight with the contained ecosystems. "Sunlight, growth, metabolism, decay," they noted, "these are the basic elements in the flow of energy through all living systems. The solar-algae ponds, as tiny ecologies, demonstrate the processes well." Measuring and calculating the effects of sunlight was not easy. Using an Eppley black-and-white pyranometer, they took seventy-two measurements of solar radiation falling on a set of tanks placed in a grassy field as well as on tanks in the solar courtyard of our newest solar bioshelter. The ensuing trigonometry calculations were complex and a closed book to those of us not involved. The team used them as the basis for a computer simulation program to predict the yearly amount of sunlight entering the ponds in the solar courtyard. The internal chemistry of the ponds was Dave's area of expertise. Besides sunlight, the other major inputs of energy into the solar-algae ponds were fish feeds and bubbled air. Water temperature, oxygen levels, and pH were measured regularly, and the evolution of the ecosystem was closely monitored. Gradually, the team was able to quantify, interpret, and document the biological complexities of the ponds.

It fell to John Wolfe to calculate the broader energetics of the solar-algae ponds. To do so, the energy used not only in operating but in manufacturing the tanks had to be weighed against the solar heat and fish protein produced. Using a concept of embodied energy flow developed at the Center for Advanced Computation at the University of Illinois, John was able to calculate the energetics of producing fish protein in our tanks within a wide spectrum of protein-producing methods. We came out very well. Our energy consumption was higher than uncooked grains, but competitive with eggs, lower than milk production, and much lower than meat. "We see that solar-algae ponds," John concluded, "offer a unique solution to the problem of creating protein in an increasingly energy scarce world."

Ron summarized their findings in lay terms: "The solar-algae ponds have several uses in greenhouse or bioshelter design. Indoors they provide a means for passive solar energy collection and for fish raising. They can be used to provide fish waste nutrients for agriculture when tank water is used for irrigation, reducing the threat of thermal shock to plant roots by pre-warming the water. The research and daily contact with these aquatic systems has increased our knowledge and perspective of the nature of ecosystems. It is also bringing us closer to understanding the dynamics and sensitivity of the biosphere of which we are all a part."

The next step was to integrate growing hydroponic vegetables on the surface of the water into solar-algae pond management. In this Ron was joined by talented aquaculturist Carl Baum. At first they were disconcerted to find that bumper vegetable crops seemed to be balanced by a slight falling off in fish growth. The plants were obviously thriving on fish wastes but also were consuming some of the nutrients. It was an issue the team was referring to as "the nutrient economy of the hydroponic ecosystem." By fine-tuning both the technology and the nutrient balance, they began moving toward a more balanced yet productive system. One key to cost-effectiveness lay in using growing troughs that were inexpensive, simple to build, and easy to maintain. Creating adequate vertical support for the cucumber vines and their pound-size fruits, while still allowing adequate light for the tomatoes and surface area for king-size heads of lettuce, was another design challenge. Overall, though, they found that a healthy plant biomass would maintain water quality and that nutrient efficiency significantly improved the economics of integrated fish and vegetable production. Carl concluded: "We are enthusiastic about the possibilities of hydroponic gardening as a vital component to a bioshelter food production scheme."

By the early 1980s, with cutbacks in federal grants, the prospect of National Science Foundation funds eventually coming to an end loomed large. This served to spur our aquaculture buffs to take advantage of whatever time they had left. With Ron at the helm, they geared themselves for a bold next step—fish production on a commercial scale. To this end, they dug what initially looked like two enormous outdoor ponds. Although they occupied only a tenth of an acre each, the sight of two shimmering ponds where we were used to seeing a field probably exaggerated their size. The idea was to expand year-round productivity by integrating the indoor solar-algae ponds with the new outdoor ponds. Ron's team intended to grow the fish to fingerling size indoors during the winter. When it was warm enough in the spring, they would transfer the fish outside to reach edible size and reproduce. A fish weighing from 5 ounces to 8 ounces was deemed appropriate size for the frying pan.

With the larger ponds we planned to compare the effectiveness of the monoculture of blue tilapia (*Sarotherodon aureus*) with a polyculture comprised of blue tilapia and Israeli carp (*Cyrprinus carpio*), a variety of common carp. Later we planned to introduce ducks to fertilize the pond by providing a nutrient base for aquatic microbial life-forms. Over the next three years we hoped to analyze this comprehensive aquatic ecosystem and to build a mathematical model of pond dy-

Solar-algae ponds in the field.

namics. From there we could go on to develop simple, optimal management techniques for fish production. Integrating this program with the agricultural work, we intended to create a commercial-scale methodology for regional food production.

The summer of 1984 turned out to be excellent for growing fish. Ron and his team triumphed with a bumper crop of more than 400 pounds of fish, not counting the few that were lost to—or shared with—a great blue heron and the occasional illicit youthful fisherman. Working with a polyculture of blue tilapia and common carp, Ron alternated the venue of the fish seasonally, wintering them in the solar-algae ponds in the bioshelters and having them spend the summer in the big outdoor ponds. Beyond adding lime to correct the excessive acidity of the pH in the outdoor ponds in the spring, once the fish had been transferred, he left them to a regime of self-management. The water level was replenished only by rain, and Ron did not attempt aeration. At harvest time everyone who sampled the fish agreed that the taste was delicious. Like the gardeners of that period, Ron and his team were also developing a market for their fish, both fresh and smoked, in local restaurants and at the Woods Hole Saturday market.

With that season's abundance, it seemed that another New Alchemy aquaculture program had achieved its goal. With this integration of Western and traditional Chinese methods that Ron had studied while traveling in Asia a few years earlier, Ron thought that 1984's harvest was probably close to the upper limit that could be achieved without a heavier technological input such as aeration in the outdoor ponds. Although he would have preferred a higher ratio of larger to smaller fish, Ron felt he had at last achieved peak production. New Alchemy had learned how to produce significant quantities of high-quality protein and had demonstrated the economic feasibility of doing so. For better or for worse, however, beyond striving to keep costs low, we never fully tested the economics of growing tilapia as a source of income for ourselves. Now, however, tilapia can be found in supermarkets and fish stores all across the United States and Canada.

Ron summed up the goals for New Alchemy's solar aquaculture as follows: "The overall objective is to develop a regionally based, economically viable fish farm that links solar and earthen pond aquaculture with agriculture and animal husbandry." Step-by-step, we had demonstrated how and why it could be done. Yet as Ron himself had acknowledged, 1984's work had brought the program to a culmination of sorts. We had long since demonstrated the viability of aquatic protein production and the low-cost creation and maintenance of prolific aquatic ecosystems. He had advanced the integration of Eastern and Western methods and brought the system to peak capacity. New Alchemy's original goals for aquaculture had been more than met. When National Science Foundation support ended due to lack of funding, the staff of New Alchemy at that time decided to terminate its aquaculture program.

However practical this may have been, many people were deeply angry or unhappy about it. Aquaculture had been integral to New Alchemy tradition and identity from the beginning. But the program seemed increasingly unlikely to find support. In addition, in the intervening years, the Institute had undergone a radical restructuring. As Kate Eldred, who was then the group scribe and editor, had observed, "The break in continuity was painful, embarrassing, and to many people, inexplicable." To them, to drop this aspect of the work, to overlook the elemental presence of the water, was a violation. Some people saw abandoning the aquaculture program as a betrayal of New Alchemy's fundamental mission, and they were slow to forgive its omission. Ron saw no further role for himself at the Institute and moved on to international consulting. Nonetheless, history has borne out that the aquaculture program, and the foundation of ecological design to which it gave rise, was New Alchemy's singular scientific achievement. As Ron had once said of his solar-algae ponds, "They're a pulsing, wild primordial soup— a little ecosystem piece of Gaia." And they were.

chapter four

Energy from the Sun, the Wind, and Conservation

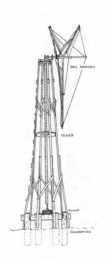

The sun on falling waters writes the text
Which yet is in the mind or in the thought.
It was a hard thing to undo this knot.
—Gerard Manley Hopkins, unfinished poem

In the mid-1970s, then as now, energy issues loomed large and were fraught with political and economic contradictions. We frequently stated in our publications that New Alchemy was a model for the feasibility of renewable energies and was therefore, by dint of its existence, an anti-nuclear statement. Most of us agreed with nuclear physicist Ted Taylor's assessment that all nuclear technologies were predicated upon human and technological infallibility. In 1975 John had encountered the renowned anthropologist Margaret Mead at Goddard College. At that time Dr. Mead had surveyed the various trappings of alternative energy on display there, very like those at New Alchemy, and commented, "This is all very fine, but none of it will be any use at all if we don't stop nuclear power!" As this served to reinforce our own uneasy feelings, we stepped up our own anti-nuclear activity and became involved with a local opposition group, the Clamshell Alliance.

The first step in active resistance for any of us from New Alchemy came in August 1976 when our membership director, Christina Rawley, was arrested at an organized nuclear protest. She was to become our most prominent anti-nuker and the link between our local group and New England and national nuclear opposition groups. In 1978 Christina,

The New Alchemy kids experimenting with solar energy. *Left to right,* Hilde's oldest son, Ate Atema (seated); a visiting child; Corinne Jacobson (in the background); Jonathan Todd; and Hilde's other sons, Sven and Jurgen Atema.

with newcomers Robert Sardinsky (who worked in New Alchemy's education and outreach programs), Gary Hirshberg (who had come to New Alchemy to apprentice with Joe Seale, our brainy physicist in residence), and our daughter Rebecca started a local Clamshell affinity group, Clams on the Half Shell.

"Clams" was made up of a mix of local supporters and a number of New Alchemists. As a group they took training in civil disobedience and became thoroughly conversant with arguments for and against nuclear energy. Clams was active at protests for several years and a number of New Alchemists, Rebecca included, had their first experience of a night in jail. Our nuclear apprehension was more than justified in March 1978 when news broke of the nuclear accident at the Three Mile Island plant in Harrisburg, Pennsylvania. A nuclear meltdown that would have affected the entire northeast was narrowly averted but radioactive contamination affected the area for years.

Building Our Windmills

Yet however essential it may have been to changing assumptions about energy use, protest and doomwatch activism was never New Alchemy's primary focus. Our research in renewable energy never proved quite as cutting-edge as our food production at New Alchemy. Where it was most innovative was in the integration of wind and solar energy into architecture and growing systems. We could hardly have claimed to be pioneers in harnessing the energy of the wind. Sailors have been doing it since time immemorial. On land windmills have been pumping water and grinding grain from the time of the great sailwings on ancient Crete. For many years water-pumping windmills were an important feature on the farms of rural America. Wind generators also filled a much needed niche in rural areas until the Rural Electrification Program centralized fossil fuel power generation in the 1940s and '50s. By the twenty-first century, although oil is still a cornerstone of the global economy, the case for renewable energy was again being made. Wind farms are now delivering electrical power reliably and cost-effectively in Germany, Denmark, Great Britain, and parts of the United States, and solar and micro-hydro power are proving themselves economically as well as environmentally. A 2004 assessment of Europe's offshore potential by the Garrad Hassan wind energy consulting group concluded that if Europe moves more aggressively to develop its vast offshore resources, wind could be supplying all of the region's residential electricity by 2020.

This level of technological advancement makes our long-ago homegrown windmills at New Alchemy look like early Wright brothers experiments beside a 757. But our windmills had great drawing power at the time. By the end of our first season, with the gardens and fishponds established, one segment of our intended tripartite research program in food, energy, and shelter was well begun. Apart from utilizing passive solar energy in the domes, however, we had not gotten very far with energy. All that was soon to change.

Word of our interest in renewable energy was out, and it began to attract some interesting new additions to New Alchemy's cast of characters. Earle Barnhart was the first of these. His Ohio farm-based family was opposed to the war in Vietnam, and Earle had written asking whether he could spend time with us as an alternative to military service. We were eager to have him but somehow, amid the summer busyness, had mislaid his letter. Fearing we had failed to protect him from being drafted, we searched frantically for the letter but never found it. But luck was with us—or with him. One afternoon I answered a knock at the farmhouse

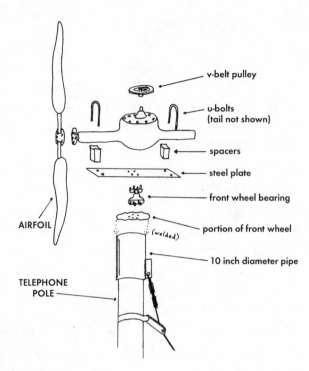

v-belt pulley

u-bolts
(tail not shown)

spacers

steel plate

front wheel bearing

portion of front wheel

(welded)

10 inch diameter pipe

AIRFOIL

TELEPHONE
POLE

Our first electricity-
generating windmill.

door. I found myself facing a muscled, bearded young man with straight brown hair cut evenly at shoulder length. Hope dawned. Could it be? Was he Earle Barnhart? Never one to waste words, Earle followed me as I led him to meet John, silent as I rattled on about how glad I was that he had found us in spite of the lost letter.

Earle was not the only less than garrulous young man to appear at the Farm about then. Attracted by rumors of experiments with wind energy, and having been involved in building windmills in India, Marcus Sherman joined the wind program not long after Earle's arrival. Cat-like and self-contained, Marcus was as at home astride the top of a windmill tower as he was on the ground.

Earle and Marcus set to work on a number of projects, including designing and building our first windmill to generate electricity. It was a high-speed, double-blade design with a mounted generator and a large propeller affixed atop a telephone pole. An old car, a Nash Rambler retired from roadwork, provided the bearing and axle mounting. Its rear differential and driveshaft unit made up the main body of the mill. It was U-bolted to a steel plate that was bolted to the pivot bearing. A belt pulley and auto alternator, battery, and regulator were harnessed for the electrical system. Blades balanced by a plywood tail rounded out the rig.

Earle and Marcus toiled on their turbine on and off throughout the summer and into the fall. Then, like the tilapia in the *New York Times*, the wind experiments had an unexpected high-profile debut. In November a producer from the British Broadcasting Corporation (BBC) contacted us. He was making a film about

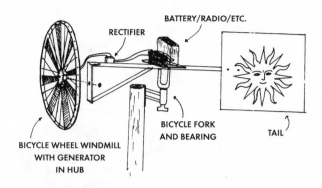

The bicycle wheel generator.

dissident scientists and wanted to see if he might find appropriate footage at the Farm. He arrived with his crew on a gray, blustery morning and found Marcus and Earle at their usual post atop their 40-foot tower. Attracted by their quixotic effort, he decided to shoot. Windblown and heroic, our energy buffs clung to the pole. As we watched and waited, the skies began to clear. After several more hours of work, Marcus and Earle climbed down and released the ropes restraining the blades. Heads tilted, we gazed upward expectantly. The cameras whirred. With a providential touch more typical of Hollywood than the BBC, the sky by then had achieved an uncompromised blue. The sun streamed down. A light wind blew, and slowly, the windmill's blades began to turn. The wind-powered blades triggered the turning of the driveshaft. This initiated the rotation of the belt pulley, which was connected to the Rambler's alternator. The alternator then converted the wind's rotational energy into electrical energy. Our windmill worked. It was a golden moment.

As the seasons passed, the energy program continued to expand. Before long, four experimental windmills dotted the rim of the hill overlooking the gardens. Slowly we were nudging a little farther along in what John Todd had called our moral obligation to substitute renewables for fossil fuel and nuclear energy. Marcus and Earle continued in their roles as inventors/engineers/mechanics/tinkers in residence. Marcus made his most lasting contribution to New Alchemy when he built a replica of the water-pumping windmill he had constructed in southern India. It was to become our prototypical and symbolic windmill. Marcus wrote of it: "Our Sailwing, with its bright red sails, has brought us an immense amount of satisfaction. With the wind passing through the rigging, one is carried off to the plains of Crete and to distant shores where men first used the wind to drive their vessels and embark upon the unknown."

Earle soon devised a second, smaller and very original electricity-generating windmill. Its most notable feature was a bicycle wheel with parallel sheet metal strips that were attached to the spokes and served as the blades. A small generator was built directly into the hub. With a square tail adorned with a painted sun, it

Mark Buchanan checking
the Savonius rotor.

produced enough power to charge batteries or, as Earle noted, run a radio or cassette player.

The third windmill, a Savonius rotor intended to pump water, was of a completely different design and appearance. Named after its Finnish inventor, it appealed to us because of the low cost and ready availability of its raw materials. It was supported by a wooden frame and made from an oil drum that had been cut in half and set on a vertical axis. Earle connected the rotor to a water pump with a reciprocating wire. The Savonius reliably pumped water up from a hand-dug well to a storage tank where it was available for use in the gardens and the fishponds. This windmill later underwent an upgrading. According to one of Earle's reports, the original steel drum version had been satisfactory for pumping groundwater into the aquaculture pond. But because it delivered only limited power, Earle replaced the steel drum wings with wings that resembled a modified letter J. In this configuration, the Savonius pumped water for the fishponds reliably for years.

More Windmills

In an article for the 1977–78 winter issue of *Wind Power Digest*, Earle Barnhart and Gary Hirshberg reported on the Sailwing, Big Red, the again improved version of Marcus's water-pumping sailwing: "The twenty-six foot tower is made of eight two by fours bolted to buried sections of telephone pole. Curved wooden buttresses add support at the base and two sets of latticework give additional sta-

Dave Engstrom working on the sailwing's blades.

bility above. A secondary platform rests approximately halfway up the tower. On top of the tower, a horizontal axle leads to the junction of three steel masts. The cloth sails are attached to the masts by grommets and pegs, like the rigging of a sailboat. Elastic shock cords connected to the adjacent mast pull the sail to form a smooth surface for catching the wind. The sail tips are attached to fixed triangular pieces at the ends of each mast. The axle and sails are oriented downwind from the tower, eliminating the need for a tail. Wind power is transferred along the rotating axle through a pair of sealed commercial bearings. A steel disc crankshaft, mounted at the base of the axle, transfers the axle rotation to the vertical motion of the pump shaft. Five distinct stroke settings are provided by holes drilled at different radii from the disc center. The assembly is centered on a steel plate turntable above the tower. The adjustable stroke disc is centered directly above a hole in the turntable, which passes through the pump shaft. From the disc, power is carried along a three-inch diameter shaft to the tire pump at ground level."

By the summer of '79, in addition to Big Red, the upgraded Savonius rotor, and an electricity-generating mill attached to our largest solar building, as well as other smaller water pumpers and circulators, there were five new windmills at work around the Farm. As Gary Hirshberg explained, "We are finding that the principal power needs in small-scale agriculture and in aquaculture are for water pumping and aeration respectively." That spring he and Joe Seale were the recipients of two windmill research grants. One grant was a contract from the U.S. Department of Energy (DOE) to construct and monitor two sailwing water-pumping windmills: a high-lift water pumper for the aquaculture unit in our newest bioshelter, and a replica of the New Alchemy sailwing to irrigate a community garden at the Christian Herter Center in Boston. This project was a first in two ways. Apart from Bill McLarney's center in Costa Rica and a more recent Canadian project on Prince Edward Island, it was the first New Alchemy project to be undertaken off-site. A windmill in central Boston would be very much in the public eye and too good an opportunity to pass up.

In undertaking to build the first New Alchemy sailwing in an urban center, Gary and his crew encountered hitches ranging from skeptical Bostonians to recalcitrant soil substrate to misplaced deliveries of cement. The target day for completion of the sailwing was Earth Day 1980, when a crowd of five thousand was expected. In an incident reminiscent of Earle and Marcus's performance for the BBC years before, Gary described his ordeal: "Hundreds of people gathered below as I climbed the tower to unfurl the mill. The crowd was hushed in anticipation. As the last bright yellow and orange sail was connected the machine began its slow, steady revolutions. All attention then focused on the water pipe below. It takes a while for a pump to develop suction but those minutes were pure agony. I climbed down and placed my hand atop the pipe to check. Slowly my hand curled inward with the pump's stroke and then exploded upward atop a tremendous surge of water. The crowd cheered and the windmill, as if encouraged by this attention, gushed forth hundreds of gallons a minute." By that time our sailwing technology had been honed to achieve a water-pumping windmill that was competitive with commercial machines in terms of performance, and could be constructed less expensively from off-the-shelf components.

Our second grant for wind research then was for a computer analysis of wind power performance The goal was to generate tables to help wind designers select the most practical match of wind rotor and end use device. According to Gary, "The designer would use the charts and a calculator to determine the best combination or rotor size, load capacity, (kilowatt or horsepower rating) and gear ratio (or stroke length and cylinder size for a water pump) to meet an average demand."

Yet for all the windmill team's advances and exploration of other possibilities, their devotion to Big Red never flagged. It continued to perform, as Gary reported, "flawlessly" circulating water through a closed-loop aquaculture raceway, pumping close to 900 gallons an hour in a 10-mile-per-hour wind. The team was still perpetually fine-tuning and improving some of its component parts. They later substituted a more durable—in our humid climate—steel tower for the original latticed wooden one. By then they were close to having completed the design for

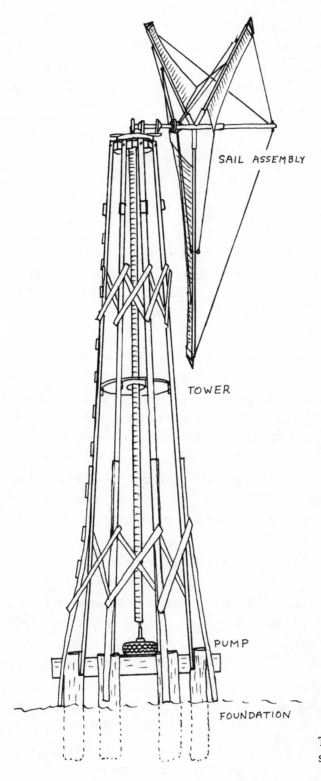

SAIL ASSEMBLY

TOWER

PUMP

FOUNDATION

The water-pumping
sailwing.

a sailwing that Gary expected could be completely constructed by a moderately skilled amateur with simple welding equipment. They concluded, "We are, overall well pleased with the New Alchemy Sailwing. It is beautiful, functional and durable. It performs well the task we ask of it. It meets the objectives we originally postulated and, in terms of cost, labor, efficiency, and usefulness, when contrasted with more standard research and development modes, it seems genuinely to qualify as an appropriate and sustainable technology."

An Energy-Conserving Conversion

Since our early days on the Farm, we had wanted to create an education center that would demonstrate state-of-the-art energy conservation and innovation. We also liked the idea of retrofitting an existing building and creating a meeting place where workshops and other events could take place in a setting that would reinforce the message of energy conservation. In the early 1980s the old dairy barn was still underutilized. The western end across the driveway from the farmhouse seemed ideal for an education center. It was perfectly suited to the kind of so-called superinsulation technologies we wanted to utilize. Superinsulation was an amalgam of construction techniques that combined energy-conscious design with, as the name indicated, massive amounts of insulation and various other new or experimental features.

We put the project in the hands of comparative newcomer Bill Smith. Bill wrote about his thoughts on the planned auditorium: "We put our problem in perspective by examining how much energy is needed for the entire heating season." His calculations of heating units (in British Thermal Units, or BTUs) indicated that the 1,500-square-foot space would require the equivalent of 137 gallons of heating fuel a year. Taking body heat from the building's occupants into consideration, he speculated, "If we remember that people will usually be in the space (radiating 400 BTUs an hour when sitting still) we can see that a mere twenty-six people can keep this building very comfortable on the coldest day of the year." With this in mind he began to seriously consider doing without an auxiliary heating system—wood, oil, or electric—altogether.

Bill and his crew of staff, volunteers, and apprentices maintained characteristic New Alchemy momentum on the job, and in a matter of months they completed the transformation of a dilapidated corner of the barn to a state-of-the-art energy education center. The three major components were airtight construction, superinsulation, and an air-to-air heat exchanger to maintain indoor air quality. Instead of a central heating system, they substituted pulses of warmth from body heat and lightbulbs. There were other backup subelements involved as well. The window glass encased a transparent film that reflected radiant heat. An instantaneous water heater warmed water only to the volume and temperature required. Wall-mounted electric heaters heated objects and people before heating the air. The toilets were low-flush. Bill emphasized that the still conventional appearance of the barn demonstrated that virtually any style of building could be adapted and retrofitted to be extremely energy efficient. This metamorphosis from leaky barn corner to energy-efficient auditorium represented our most literal attempt in the transformation of shelter at that time and was a harbinger of advances yet to come elsewhere.

Back in New Alchemy's day, as now, dark shadows hovered over both nuclear technologies and fossil fuel–driven economies. One that was to shape the course of not only the Institute but the future of John Todd's work in ecological design had emerged from the oil embargo by OPEC (Organization of Petroleum Exporting Countries) back in 1973. The energy crisis, as it came to be called, caused a great deal of inconvenience, as those who had to wait in line for gas and worry about soaring prices will remember. Unintentionally, it also gave environmentalists a unique educational window to emphasize the folly of excessive dependence on foreign oil and made the potential of renewables seem less whimsical to the general public. At the time of the embargo John attended a conference and returned with new and far-reaching insights based on the energy analysis of ecologist Howard Odum. Dr. Odum's groundbreaking Report to the Royal Swedish Academy, entitled *Energy, Ecology, and Economics*, clearly delineated the dangers inherent in fossil fuel–driven dependence for industrial economies. It made clear the pervasiveness of such reliance throughout the entire infrastructure of these economies, which the turmoil in the Middle East and the war in Iraq have since robustly substantiated. Fueled with valuable new information, environmentalists back then seized upon the Odum report as a wake-up call and made widespread use of it.

Relevant as we found Dr. Odum's analysis of energy systems, we considered his ideas on the relationship between human societies and the natural world even more catalytic. His thinking profoundly influenced John and, eventually, the discipline of ecological design. Howard Odum maintained that nature, in a way, could be viewed as a vast bin of spare parts, which were available for integrating into human support systems. This thinking, John saw, could be harnessed to create adaptive technologies to serve human needs. Already inclined in that direction, John and Earle particularly were stimulated to become more innovative in their design strategies. They observed the natural world even more closely, turning to it as a resource not to be mined or raped, but rather to be studied, consulted, and imitated. Bolstered by the Odum report, New Alchemy stepped more confidently along on the path of coevolution with the natural world. As John explained: "By passing through the portals of nature, we can begin to work with or through her so that scars begin to heal. The path will involve the three strands of practicality, science on a small and human scale, and a wisdom that is philosophical, even mystical."

chapter five

Education and Outreach

The individual mind is immanent but not only in the body. It is immanent also in messages and passages outside the body: and there is a larger Mind of which the individual mind is only a sub-system. This larger mind is comparable to God and is perhaps what some people mean by God, but it is still immanent in the total interconnected social system and planetary ecology.
—Gregory Bateson, *Form, Substance, and Difference*

From its inception we had intended New Alchemy to serve not only as a research institute but as a self-designated educational organization. Typically, like most of our programs, our education projects were unorthodox and largely self-organizing. Underlying what could frequently seem a party-like atmosphere among us, there was always a sense of urgency to share what we were doing beyond the immediate group. "To inform the earth's stewards" was, after all, part of our ethical underpinnings. As soon as we moved out to the Farm, we started to have visitors, especially on Saturdays. Most of them were eager to participate in some way. Casting about for a mutually agreeable and efficient way to organize them, we evolved a loose structure for managing the day.

The staff and core group would arrive early, bringing kids and food, and divide ourselves among the projects to be tackled. These could range from assorted garden chores to tending fishponds to building domes. The idea was that visitors would gravitate to whatever most interested them. The system worked beautifully, and we got an amazing amount done. As Saturdays expanded to involve long hours of work, the necessity for providing some kind of lunch became obvious. A potluck arrangement seemed the only workable option. Word spread quickly, even without e-mail, and almost everyone began to bring food. At around noon we would set up the assemblage of dishes on outside tables behind the house and let people serve themselves. The fare varied wildly. Some of us were attempting to make a subliminal statement about the connections between health and nutrition and the benefits of organic, homegrown, or local food. Hilde Maingay and I usually felt a maternal obligation to provide quantity and sound nutrition. We tended to concentrate on organic bean or rice salads or yogurt dishes with fresh fruit, which our kids usually shunned in favor of less stolid offerings. Vegetarians came bearing everything from the most exquisitely prepared dishes to large, untreated, tooth-challenging servings of raw vegetables and slabs of tofu. There were, of course, those who chose to tweak the well intentioned and appeared with large platters of salami, ham, sausage, and other frowned-upon delicatessen offerings. Most popular of all, of course, were those bearing desserts. Carrot cake with cream cheese icing became a tradition.

Saturday lunches quickly became one of the social high points of the week. New Alchemists and visitors would picnic together on the grass, some settling in a large uneven circle, some in scattered groups. It was almost always enjoyable, sometimes uproarious, and often characterized by very good conversation. There was informative, even brilliant, discussion when people such as appropriate technology guru E. F. Schumacher, the author of *Small Is Beautiful*; educator John Holt; Whole Earth publications founder Stewart Brand; or astronaut Rusty Schweikart joined us for lunch. When the time came to return to work, we all trouped over to a large pot filled with fire-heated water and did our own dishes. Leaving a dirty dish for someone else to wash was frowned upon. Some of the Saturday visitors became regulars.

In those days before e-mail and the Internet, we never quite understood how word of New Alchemy was spreading so rapidly, but we were delighted to have such a great number of visitors to our Farm. Some of those who stopped by became friends, and, as Isak Dinesen noted in *Out of Africa,* "The visits of my friends to the farm were happy events in my life and the farm knew it." Once we got over being somewhat incredulous at how many people were taking what we were doing seriously, it greatly reinforced our confidence in our mission.

With each year we saw an increase not only in the numbers of visitors but also in the segments of the culture they represented. After the predominance of the long-haired or bearded young in the early days of the Institute, visitors were now becoming harder to categorize. We were seeing families, some with small chil-

Lunch on Farm Saturday. *Foreground, starting with man in hat, continuing to the right around the circle,* hatted visitor, Susan Ervin, Ruth Hubbard Wald, George Wald, Nancy Todd, E. F Schumacher, Ian Baldwin, and another visitor. *At far left, behind circle,* Don Estes and Ty Cashman. *Identifiable in the background,* Hilde Maingay and John Todd (both blonde), Bryce Butler (bearded), and Bill McLarney with visitors.

dren, some with teenagers, and some with grandparents. Garden clubs made up of older people stopped by, as did classes of schoolchildren and, sometimes, an entire small school. There were also homesteaders, students of all kinds, would-be dropouts from business and academe, tinkers, lovers of windmills, and anyone else in search of a gentler approach to life.

By the time the average number of visitors on a given Saturday had risen beyond seventy, it became clear we would have to offer a more organized format for the day. It was no longer adequate just to answer questions in the gardens or over lunch, and there simply were not enough of us to make this workable any longer. After much discussion, we adopted the tactic of "the tour." It had already started in an informal and spontaneous way when, at times, a group of people would gather around one or another of us as we were working to ask questions or request explanations. This expanded and became more mobile until it literally was a tour. It would begin before lunch with one of us banging a gong to summon everyone to the lawn behind the house, which had tacitly become the accustomed gathering place. Then one of us would lead off with a general introduction before

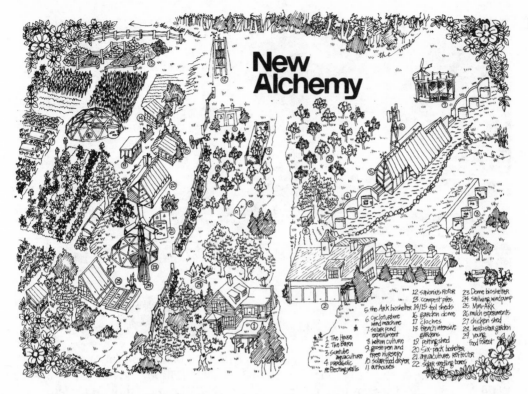

Map of the New Alchemy Farm.

setting off on a circuit that would feature stops at all the major installations, where one or several of us would offer more extended descriptions of the work in progress. Most visitors seemed pleased enough and, kids included, trouped around gamely. Soon the tour became an institution, as much a part of those Saturdays as the work sessions that had preceded it or the potluck feast that followed.

By 1975, even with the tour, we again felt we were not doing as much as we could in the way of outreach. The crowds were becoming too unwieldy to be squeezed into the dome or the other structures without mishap to the fish, the plants, or one of the visitors. We actually did have an unfortunate incident one Saturday with a woman who had arrived late. Barely breaking stride as she approached the reception area behind the house, she peremptorily demanded where she should join the tour. A bit startled—brusqueness was not our style—we indicated the crowd then filing into the dome, and off she dashed once again. As luck would have it, the surface of the dome pond was thickly carpeted with a layer of vibrantly green duckweed.

Before any of us could collect ourselves and voice a warning, our fast-moving visitor had achieved the dome, overshot the pond's perimeter, and disappeared beneath the surface of the water. Almost as quickly as she had arrived, she reemerged, dripping, from the dome. Struggling not entirely successfully to maintain our composure and refrain from sniggering, several of us headed inside to rummage for dry clothes for her. One more indication, we decided, of the need for improved management of the flow of visitors.

Our next tactic for Farm Saturdays was to offer a series of workshops. This, we hoped, would give people a general background and then free them to pursue particular interests in depth. Under this regime we still started at noon with a general introduction and the ever-eclectic potluck lunch. The workshop topics covered our research in agriculture, aquaculture, energy, and bioshelters. The specific subjects varied somewhat from week to week; pest resistance, agricultural forestry, or intensive cultivation could be covered under the rubric of agriculture. Workshops in aquaculture and energy were always well attended. Christina Rawley and I usually held an additional workshop devoted to the larger social change of which we at the Institute saw ourselves a part, with topics ranging from feminism to environmental education to nuclear opposition. Most of the workshop leaders usually succeeded in making their sessions genuine discussions rather than lectures, and generally a fair amount was learned all around.

Evolving Education Programs

As time passed, although we were still sticking to the general introduction/potluck lunch/tour/workshop format, we were aware that we were offering up a broad palette and some of us were feeling uneasy about the clarity of our message. Perhaps we needed a more comprehensive educational program to make the ideas accessible to and exciting for both adults and children. With the arrival of tall, dark-haired Rob "Sardo" Sardinsky, we found the right person for the job. Sardo was an imaginative vegetarian cook, a committed anti-nuclear activist, and an enthusiastic educator.

Sun Day of May 1978 was internationally designated for promoting a solar future. At Sardo's initiative we invited over six hundred students from the Cape's regional schools to tour the Farm. More than a thousand people turned up. Sardo wrote of that day: "I showed two elementary classes and one high school class around the Farm. My first two tours were with groups of first and third graders who were as excited as Mexican jumping beans, curious about almost everything, and full of thought-provoking questions. New Alchemy took on a completely different perspective for me as I saw it through their eyes."

The success of that Sun Day triggered a significant demand from other school groups. The following October, Sardo launched a one-year feasibility program to determine whether the Farm could be used for classes for school groups without

A group of visiting schoolchildren at one of the garden sheds.

interfering with our work. He was also exploring whether and how such a program could be sustained financially. That summer we also conducted a federally sponsored training program in landscaping and gardening for local teenagers. The Comprehensive Employment and Training Act (CETA) provided grants to state and local governments for job training and youth programs. The new teenagers added even more diversity to the already mixed group around the Farm.

That mixed bunch included many volunteers who did not turn up only on Saturdays to help out. For these volunteers, information gathering and assimilation was completely informal. Not long after Earle Barnhart arrived, he was joined in his wind research by Mark Buchanan, the first African American to work with us for any length of time. Mark was also our pioneer apprentice or intern. From his partnership with Earle emerged a program that became central to our evolution. Over the years several hundred people, usually young, signed on with a particular staff member to gain knowledge and experience in projects that interested them. For many years the apprentice program was an informal process, loosely self-organizing but somehow effective. It is hard to know how word spread in those days, but, as was the case with Saturday visitors, we consistently attracted many bright, idealistic young people. Many were college students taking time off or changing the focus of their studies. Others were more hands-on than academic in their inclinations and wanted experience in the fields we were researching. Many liked the idea of greater self-sufficiency. A number were no longer young but attracted by New Alchemy's message and interested in seeing if it could be integrated into their own lives. It was a mutually beneficial arrangement. The apprentices or interns—the terms were mutually exchangeable—received education and training not widely available elsewhere, and we gained much needed help in carrying our ever-growing workload.

When Sardo moved on, Greg Watson took his place. Greg was a bit of an anomaly. He was an African American environmentalist at a time when the political energy and idealism of most blacks was tied up in fighting racism. Charming and gregarious, he was also an intellectual and a devotee, in equal parts, of maverick inventor Buckminster Fuller and of baseball. As education director, Greg's first effort in outreach was to give our ideas a higher profile in the immediate community. He initiated the first New Alchemy Annual Run for the Sun, an event that attracted local runners and other newcomers to the Farm and indirectly called attention to the promise of renewable forms of energy. He also introduced a series of more intensive workshops to the established Farm Saturday program. For a fee of $35 per person we offered daylong Saturday courses in tree crops, year-round gardening, wind systems, aquaculture in solar ponds and in lakes, and women and appropriate technology.

Writing, Publishing, and Speaking Out

Concomitant to our efforts in on-site educational outreach were our ongoing attempts to communicate with people who were not likely to be spending much time with us at the Farm. In retrospect, New Alchemy's publishing program (although calling it that would have seemed ridiculously overblown at the time) was actually our first deliberate effort in outreach. It emerged back in San Diego as John, Bill, and I were slowly piecing together disparate bits of information and striving for a more comprehensive understanding of the social/environmental dynamic. At the same time we realized that if anything was to come of our ideas, we needed to test them more broadly. To do so, it became a priority to reach out to other like-minded people and organizations. During that period John wrote an article that we self-published in pamphlet form that he called, in homage to Jonathan Swift, "A Modest Proposal" with the subtitle "Humanity's Future Is Threatened by a Loss of Biological and Social Diversity. To Counter This, a New Biotechnology Is Proposed." (The term *biotechnology* was then a neutral word without the current connotations of genetic manipulation with the goal of maximizing corporate profits.)

In "A Modest Proposal," John reported on the disturbing phenomena we had been learning about. At the time of his writing, many of the problems that are now more widely acknowledged were largely unforeseen. The green revolution was still being hailed as the panacea for a hungry world. The lack of diversity in agriculture or in ecosystems had not been seen as threatening. The energy crisis of 1973 was still to come. Genetic engineering was not part of public consciousness.

John proposed a number of measures he said could lead to a more promising future. He wrote of the imperative "to create biologically based technologies based upon an ecological ethic. It would function," he explained, "at the lowest levels of society, providing inexpensive life-support bases for individual families, small farmers, or communities who desire more independence and a way of life that restores rather than destroys this fragile planet. It would be founded on the philosophical view that all things are interconnected and interdependent, and that the whole cannot be defined in monetary terms. Energy production, agriculture, landscapes, and communities must be tied together within individual research programs and each area should be considered as a unique entity worthy of study. From indigenous research projects would evolve a biotechnology that reflects the needs of each region and peoples. In this way it will be possible to have fantastically varied communities and landscapes, as each develops its own integration with the world around it." Unexpectedly, "A Modest Proposal" proved to be a modest shot that was heard around the world. Widely read and distributed, it was translated into Japanese and almost all the European languages. It was and is the best expression of New Alchemy's philosophy and purpose at the time of its founding and is, if anything, even more relevant today.

Nonprofit organizations such as New Alchemy, in order to maintain tax-exempt status, are required to issue some form of report to supporters, contributors, and members at least once a year. We were both willing and eager to comply. Subsequent to "A Modest Proposal," our publications were variously called newsletters and bulletins. They fulfilled our legal obligation and effectively launched our message, but they had been rather piecemeal and sporadic efforts.

Our first high point in terms of publishing was not actually a New Alchemy venture, however, although we still bathed unashamedly in its reflected glory. Ever since our California days, in the little time he could spare away from his fish and music, Bill had been toiling away on an ancient typewriter. His project, co-authored by John Bardach and John Ryther, came to fruition in the late summer of 1973 when Wiley Interscience published his book, *Aquaculture: The Farming and Husbandry of Freshwater Organisms*. This book was quickly recognized as filling a much-needed historic, scientific, and information gap in the literature and remains the most substantive text in the field. It was nominated for a National Book Award in 1974.

That same year brought another publishing debut in the form of the *Journal of the New Alchemists*. It was to be the first of seven issues. Although I had been involved in the writing and editing of our earlier publishing efforts, it was with the *Journal* that I took on full responsibility for the publishing program and assumed the mantle of editor and group scribe. This, in turn, more sharply delineated my place within the group. Editing the work of friends can be hard, even painful, for both writer and editor. But producing the *Journal*s was, for me, a labor of love. I now had a chance to hold up a mirror to the people and the work to which I was utterly committed, and to reflect that vision to the larger world. Writing and editing suited me well not only because I enjoyed it, but because I could work at home much of the time and be there when the kids came home from school or when colds or flu struck.

Our earlier publications, like ourselves while still in a formative stage, had been somewhat makeshift in appearance as well as timing. With the *Journal*s we hit upon a style and format that worked, and, with a few modifications, we stayed with it. To find a printer who could help us achieve this, in those long-ago days before desktop publishing, John and I had driven up the Cape one raw, wet, winter afternoon to meet Jack Viall, a printer with a honed, New England aesthetic. He turned out to be the perfect ally. He suggested that we aim for a cross between a book and a magazine, bound and just over eight by eleven inches in size. To create a feeling that would be both earthy and distinctive—a bit evocative of old-fashioned sepia prints—Jack advised we try ecru-colored paper and dark brown ink. We trusted him, and he produced a beautiful volume in which we could take genuine pride.

The first *Journal* was illustrated in a quasi-medieval style adapted from the Book of Kells and contained no photographs. Hilde Maingay, who has a gift for capturing the moment, contributed most of the photos that added credibility, humor, and charm to successive *Journal*s. The bulk of the written content was made up of reports on the various programs of the preceding year, compiled by the people involved. This was rounded out with anecdotes, sketches, comments from the kids, poetry, and quotations from whatever some of us were reading or studying at the time. The *Journal* was expensive to produce, but we were willing as a group to scrape together the money to do so because the publication seemed to ring so true to the times. Like the *Whole Earth Catalog*, the Beatles, or the songs of Bob Dylan, the *Journal* seemed to hit exactly the right note. It was included as part of the membership program and was also sold separately from the office on Farm Saturdays and through the mail.

The contents of the *Journal*s were divided under five main subsections: "New Alchemy," "Energy," "Land and Its Use," "Aquaculture," and "Explorations." Although the titles were largely self-explanatory, they were, we thought, as logical

Last journal of the
New Alchemists.

a rubric as any for reporting on the work. Yet all were parts of a greater whole. "Even more important than the divisions we have created," I wrote in that first issue, "is the underlying unity of the work and the ideas. The view we wish to share is holistic rather than fragmented. Echoing many voices, recording our research, reflecting broader experiences as we travel the world or as the world touches us, we plan to share with our Associates and readers and friends as much of New Alchemy as can be transmitted onto paper."

Now, like the acceptance of organic agriculture generally, the emphasis on food that is not only organic but seasonal and locally grown has become widespread. It was less so when, in the third and fourth *Journals*, under the title "The Cook Book of the New Alchemists," we wrote extensively about our thinking on food. "At New Alchemy we have always felt that work with food is work to be honored. To have enough food in a hungry world, to have access to land and to grow some of one's own food in a commercialized culture is to be privileged. To nourish people one cares for and yet to leave the soil undepleted is a gratifying and fulfilling aspect of the human experience." In our Cook Book we offered some of our many recipes for dried beans, cabbage and sour cream pie, fish and vegetable curry, zucchini casserole, vegetarian moussaka, and assorted stir-fries, soups, salads, and breads. Those were, Susan Ervin reported, "some of the good things we made."

In the third *Journal* I voiced some of my own preoccupations in an article called "Women and Ecology." Reviewing the deteriorating state of planetary ecology, I speculated on the potential role for women attempting to redress the balance. In our earlier publications we had more than once used an image of the hermetic androgyne, a symbol of traditional alchemy. The androgyne—a man/woman—was portrayed as a single figure, half-female, half-male, with separate heads and a conjoined body. At once man and woman, king and queen, it was often depicted standing on the brow of a dragon. In Chinese alchemy the dragon represented the forces of nature. By sheer coincidence—or some subconscious manifestation of the Tao—we had hit upon a key to fundamental and essential transformation: a balance of masculine and feminine principles rooted inseparably in the natural world, equal partners in seeking to right the balance of the human relationship to that world. The ultimate alchemy.

Actualizing that balance, however, took a certain amount of recalibrating on all our parts. Although some of our work was still divided along traditional lines, the transition to equal sharing of the tasks we found most oppressive psychologically was weathered with very little rancor. Group clean-ups usually resembled a cheerful brawl more closely than housework, but the results were adequate and the karma was fine. We women also seized the chance to explore and acquire a number of new skills, including carpentry, construction, and even car repair. Some of us became very good at what we tried. But through disheartening trial and error, I discovered my talents lie steadfastly in traditional women's areas. Realizing this still left me feeling remiss at not broadening my range and tackling some new challenge. Searching for a niche less silent than editor, I examined the profile we presented as an institute to the outside world.

John and Bill McLarney, although very different, were both articulate and charismatic and projected an image that was radical and compelling. But being male, they did not fully reflect the reality of the group. As I gathered experience on Farm Saturdays, I began to think I could expand on what I was doing there. It would be a way in which I could represent New Alchemy in the public arena and begin to balance the larger gestalt by which we were generally perceived. To become a public speaker, I had to summon the confidence to discuss scientific ideas. I argued that I had the right to do so as a representative of all who are voiceless in the face of the advances of science and technology, yet remain paradoxically its benefactors and its victims. Increasingly, as I wrote and spoke about who we were and what we were doing, New Alchemy's profile began to reflect more truly the balance we were struggling to manifest. In retrospect, we came to see that we had unwittingly and only half consciously been on this path since the beginning.

There were other issues, many of them symptomatic of the larger culture. One circled around our approach to food. In the context of feminist thinking then, the preparation of food was sometimes viewed as yet another instance of the oppression of women by men. Some of us were familiar with the equation: life = power = food. We saw this as a male conception of power, as "power *over*." In our attitude toward the growing and preparation of food, we chose to think of the inherent power of food as immanent, as "power in *being*." It was seeking to clarify these kinds of undercurrents that led me to brood on the connections between women and ecology. I still do.

One issue that troubled me then, which I think is perhaps the defining difference between my own and my daughters' generations, is that of full identity or personhood. At that time, for women, their sense of self was more societally than personally defined. An incident that took place one Farm Saturday encapsulates as well as any number of case histories the need we had to confront this conditioning. The day was enervatingly hot. Most of the group was off at a conference, leaving us with a fairly slim crew of five or six on the home front. Having done my stint at overseeing lunch, I served myself and then surveyed the area to see if there were any visitors who might be interested in having a staff person to chat with. I spotted a friendly seeming group of women picnicking in the shade of the mulberry tree. They waved me over to them, and I plunked down on the grass beside them. A pleasant-looking woman with springy gray hair smiled and scanned the rest of the staff then in evidence. Turning back to me she asked, "And who [meaning, what man] are you with?" Automatically, I looked around for John. As I did so, the scales fell from my own eyes. Shaken, I demanded: "Why do you ask me whom I'm with? Why don't you ask me who I AM?" She was as startled as I. In that one moment we had both been brought up short by the degree to which we had been programmed by society.

As we continued to integrate more of the tenets of feminism into our daily lives at New Alchemy, I took it on as my mission to tackle the issue of sexist language. I was influenced in this by the peace and feminist activist Elise Boulding, whom I had admired since my time in Ann Arbor. I had come to see the use of the generic term *man* to denote all human beings as yet another means of reinforcing the image of women as adjunct to and subservient to men. I brushed up on its etymology and learned that the word *man* has Indo-European roots in the word for "hand." The word *men* is believed to have roots in the Indo-European for "mind" or "thought." Although neither had objectionable connotations in terms of gender, it does not detract from the fact that sexist language, if less prevalent, is still very much with us. It remains the semantic tip of a cultural iceberg, a lingering malaise that ranges from habit to misogyny. It was not a trivial issue then, and it is not one now.

Pursuing my cause within the group at New Alchemy presented few difficulties. Most of us managed to segue fairly smoothly from "man," "mankind," and the omnipresent "he" to "humanity," "humankind," and some dodging or alternating of pronouns. Such is the power of the editor, I soon discovered, that any slips in our own publications were quickly righted. Whereas we originally had stated, "The New Alchemy Institute is a small international organization for research and education on behalf of man and the planet," we simply substituted "humanity" for "man." And, of course, the struggle to achieve greater parity within the group was an ongoing process. Women's caucuses and workshops became an integrated segment of our overall reality. Again, this took place with little acrimony although not always with overwhelming enthusiasm on the part of everyone. McLarney once was spotted crawling behind some conveniently located bushes to avoid encountering an empowerment workshop composed entirely of women.

Carrying my semantic campaign beyond the sympathetic confines of the group required more boldness. I decided I would not confront people publicly but speak privately to anyone I heard still using the traditional generic "man." When I heard speakers at gatherings still using "man" to refer to all of us, I approached them afterward and made my appeal. A few of them, usually older and male, were resentful or recalcitrant. Almost everyone else, when I explained that I thought to include women under the traditional generic term violated our essential sense of ourselves, reacted favorably. The cofounder of the Rocky Mountain Institute, Amory Lovins, replied simply and graciously, "Thank you."

We had no idea whether we were on the right track when we started sending the *Journals*, with their eclectic mix of writings, out into the world. Over time word trickled back to us that our message was being heard and, in some cases, acted upon. Among the most prominent of those taking it to heart were agricultural innovator Wes Jackson, cofounder of the Land Institute, and environmental educator David Orr, founder of Meadowcreek and now director of environmental studies at Oberlin College. Both of them have told us that the *Journals* inspired them to strike out on their own, in spite of financial uncertainty, and to undertake the work they felt most urgently needed to be done. (The assumption that if we could do it, anyone could, was only implied.) As part of an evaluation of our work for the Rockefeller Brothers Fund, its scientific advisor, Dr. Barry Valentine, admitted, "Frankly, when I first heard about the New Alchemists, I was so turned off by the name that I did not take them seriously. I expected a group of ragged fanatics intent on escaping from society. Reading the fourth *Journal of the New Alchemists* marked a turning point. It was well and intelligently written, meticulously edited, and obviously produced by a dedicated and enthusiastic staff. It was clear that my first impressions were wrong."

For me, perhaps the most telling evidence of the reach of the *Journals* came many years later in 1988 when John was invited to speak at an environmental gathering in the former Yugoslavia. As the meeting began to disperse, a number of people approached me, clutching much worn and thumbed-through copies of old *Journals*. "Which one is Bill McLarney?" they would ask, pointing to one of Hilde's photographs. "Which is Earle? Does the Savonius still work?" Caught completely off-guard, I learned that the *Journals* had been a kind of lifeline for them, and I had a sudden inkling of how unknowable are the consequences of one's acts and how terrible is the responsibility to be honest.

chapter six

From Shelter to
Bioshelter to Gaia

What pattern connects the crab to the lobster and the orchid
to the primrose and all four of them to me? And me to you?
And all the six of us to amoeba in one direction and the
back ward schizophrenic in another? What is the pattern
which connects all living creatures?
—Gregory Bateson, *Mind and Nature*

A major catalyst in striking out on our own and creating New Alchemy
had been that, at the time, a cross-disciplinary approach to research
was not widely accepted. We had a hunch that integration was the crux
of it all. Even before we moved to the Farm, we had begun to experiment with integrating agriculture and aquaculture. From his study of
Asian aquaculture, Bill McLarney was familiar with the use of fishpond
water to irrigate vegetable crops, but thought there had been little sys-
tematic investigation of its effects on plants. This irrigation method
had also been used in England, at least according to Beatrix Potter.

I learned this one evening when I was reading *Peter Rabbit* to our
daughter Susannah. We had come to the part in which Peter, attempting to escape from a large white cat, hid in a watering can that Mr. Mc-
Gregor, whose garden he liked to raid, had left by a fishpond. Mr. Mc-
Gregor kept the watering can there, Beatrix Potter explained, so that
he could fill it with pond water with which he watered his vegetables.
I subsequently told Bill about Mr. McGregor, and he responded by always listing Potter, B., as a reference on all his reports. Once we had the
space out at the Farm, he set out to test Mr. McGregor's methods scientifically. Although Bill's primary focus was on aquaculture, he was
also struggling toward a deeper understanding of the aquatic and

terrestrial interactions of our various systems. Both he and John had a hunch that fishpond water might have fertilizing properties, and Bill set out to see if this was so.

After his first season of planting, watering, harvesting, weighing, and statistical analysis, Bill concluded that "irrigation with fertile fish pond water is of no particular value in growing most root and fruit crops, but it definitely enhances the growth of leaf lettuce and probably many other leaf crops, with the likely exceptions of beet greens and chard." In subsequent trials, Bill tested zucchini, beets, and Bibb lettuce. Bill and his crew set up a carefully monitored planting, watering, weeding, harvesting, and weighing regime; they kept meticulous records and later had the data statistically analyzed. His subsequent report summarized the findings as follows: "We have shown that the practice of watering with enriched fish pond water is not universally effective in increasing growth and production of garden vegetables, but we have also shown that it is effective with two varieties of lettuce. We tentatively conclude that it would be beneficial to most shallow-rooted leaf crop vegetables, particularly those which, like lettuce, favor abundant moisture and high levels of nitrogen."

For all the unorthodoxies that abounded at New Alchemy, one area in which we were absolutely disciplined and precise was in the conduct of our research. Where we differed from mainstream science was in our focus on sustainability, protection, and restoration—and in freedom from the corporate funding that controls so much scientific inquiry. Otherwise Bill and John and their colleagues understood only too well that any scientific casualness on our part could undermine and betray underlying goals of the Institute. One aspect to our research that was ongoing for the duration of the Institute was the observation and recording of data and phenomena. In order to substantiate our progress in the nature-based science we were exploring, we carefully monitored every system, biological and technical, to give us an accurate understanding of the efficacy of our experiments and a better grasp of conditions under which various ideas might be transplanted to other environments. This put us in a better position to advise people about trying to raise tilapia in their area, for example, or whether or not they would need an enclosed area to extend the growing season.

Bob Angevine kept records of the weather, including the amount of rainfall received at the site. As our various bioshelters were developed, Earle Barnhart took on the task of tracking the internal climates of our biological systems and recording the data, as well as checking air and water temperatures, humidity, and the turbidity of the water in the fishponds. Earle also kept an eye on the windmills, generally evaluating performance and noting such things as pumping rates in relation to wind speed. In connection to his aquaculture projects, Bill was also involved in recording and calculating, often painstakingly, his experiments with using fishpond water as a nutrient source for vegetables and his home-grown fish foods.

Knowledge of the biochemistry in all the aquaculture systems was seen as vital. John regularly measured oxygen, nitrogen, carbon, and phosphorous cycles so that any imbalance could be detected and corrected. He watched algae production and studied the systems with regard to their ability to maintain clean water in the fish culture ponds. As a result of his observations, we introduced both microscopic and flowering plants for water purification as well as for fish food. Even the garden was subject to scientific scrutiny. Hilde Maingay had to track the chemistry of the soil and evaluate various combinations in companion planting, seasonal fluxes, and the results of mulching and composting. Susan Ervin launched a study of the feasibility of using mosquito fish (*Gambusia* spp.) in mosquito control and similarly had to record her findings. It was her monitoring of fluctuating insect populations and damage in the gardens that eventually led us to explore integrated pest management. Daily and yearly we collected data that were later pondered and eventually applied, as the requisite measuring, recording, testing, and weighing were systematically woven into our rounds.

The purpose behind all the monitoring and data collection was to achieve further integration and tighter links between growing food, producing and conserving energy, and exploring innovative forms of shelter. The consumption of fossil fuel in standard agriculture—not only in transportation but also in the application of fertilizers, pesticides, and herbicides—is a major source of chemical contamination, carcinogens, and endocrine disrupters. We saw linking food growing and renewable energy as a path toward greater energy efficiency. Our efforts to integrate them into shelter began with the domes we erected over and around fishponds.

Our reasoning in tackling issues of shelter lay in the fact that, throughout the industrial world, almost all houses—or dwellings of any kind—are net consumers of resources. Most houses require, after initial construction, enormous inputs in the form of utilities, provisions, and all the other consumer items most of us find necessary in running a household. The major outputs are pollution and waste. This is not sustainable in the long run. We felt that anything we could do to balance that equation would be a step in the right direction. The first successors to the dome in our front yard were the two we built over the aquaculture ponds at the Farm in sessions akin to old-fashioned barn raisings. Because domes had a propensity to leak, our main conclusion from our experiments with shelter at this stage was best summarized by Bill's declaration that "domes belong over fish ponds." In spite of this, they served as season extenders for both the warm water–loving tilapia and the vegetables we grew around the rim of the ponds. The domes sheltered our early integration of food growing with solar energy collection and storage and laid the groundwork for the more sophisticated greenhouses or bioshelters that were to come.

Launching the Arks

As our research in shelter advanced beyond those early domes, we were hatching more ambitious plans. In 1974 we converted a rather primitive shack-like structure, which was our first solar structure that was not a dome, to what was called a Miniature Ark or Mini-Ark. It completed the assemblage of solar buildings and windmills—our technology row—on the ridge overlooking the garden. The Mini-Ark was designed to test the effectiveness of water flow, rapid nutrient exchange, and biopurification in a small, closed aquaculture facility. The primary energy inputs were the sun and the wind, which not only provided light and heat but pumped water. The Mini-Ark's most important role, however, lay in testing biological and energy strategies for a full-scale bioshelter, which we hoped to design and build in order to achieve further linkages among horticulture, aquaculture, energy, and architecture.

These new experimental structures, at John's suggestion, were to become known as Arks. The name seemed appropriate. Noah's Ark had survived the biblical flood to provide a source of creatures to start life over again, and we intended our bioshelters to harbor a wide and resilient variety of life-forms. Should the need arise, our Arks could also serve as incubators for reestablishing depleted biological resources. We were conceptualizing an Ark/bioshelter not only for the Farm, but with a fairly concrete assurance of funding from the Canadian government, a second structure for Prince Edward Island in the Maritimes.

All of us were involved in pooling design ideas for the Arks. Hilde and Earle organized and evaluated the multiple components and integrated them into a basic design plan. At that stage it became obvious that we needed more architectural skills than any of us could muster. Hilde's fellow gardener Nancy Willis suggested we pool resources with David Bergmark and Ole Hammarlund, a freewheeling pair of young architects who called their firm Solsearch. The New Alchemy/ Solsearch combination proved symbiotic. David and Ole, both tall, bearded, and given to wearing clogs, delved into biology, energy conservation, and appropriate technologies. We boned up on architectural theory. Our first shared project was to build a prototype bioshelter at the Farm to test some of the materials and technologies, particularly light-transmitting materials, to be ready when the projected Canadian funding came through.

Building the Ark became possible sooner than we had dared hope through a grant from the Jessie Smith Noyes Foundation. The president of the New York–based foundation, Edith Muma, made her initial visit one August day with her husband and partner, John Muma. On their tour of the Farm they overlooked nothing and asked questions at all stops. Johnny, an engineer, fell in love with the windmills and was up and down every tower, checking details and comparing notes with Earle, John, and Ty Cashman. By the time lunch was over, we had formed the basis of a lifelong friendship. Edie was later to tell us that day changed her life. She wrote of how she had seen that "ideas could be made real when there was true caring and true vision. I saw how this would change the future, one person at a time, not by copying it but by providing the foundation of their future lives." With Johnny's unequivocal approval, Edie arranged for a Noyes Foundation grant for New Alchemy to design and build an Ark on the Cape that would be a sister ship for the Prince Edward Island bioshelter.

The Arks were to be a logical extension of New Alchemy's work to date. The process of designing them brought us to a conceptual watershed. We were confronted with whether, in terms of New Alchemy philosophy, we wanted to incorporate the use of computers into our overall design strategies. The idea of electronic monitors for the various biological systems in the Arks was introduced by newcomer Al Doolittle, who was one of the first generation of trained computer programmers and had come to us on the advice of his research adviser at the Yale School of Forestry and Environmental Studies. He had been using minicomputers to study the effects of air pollution on forest growth, and had designed and built a portable laboratory that could be used in the field to monitor respiration rates of trees exposed to pollutants. He came to New Alchemy because, in his words, "I felt the microcomputer could be used as a tool to democratize science. By making the tools used by scientists accessible to those that did not have huge research grants, scientific studies of ecological and agricultural alternatives would have an equal voice with studies from the mainstream scientific community." He proposed that electronic monitoring be used in the bioshelters because it would greatly enhance our ability to understand and maximize the effectiveness of the structures. Some of us took convincing. Computers were not then integral to almost all forms of work, as they are now, and we probably had a slightly Luddite suspicion that they were too high-tech for our biological, hands-on approach. Earle Barnhart thought that they would be acceptable when used as monitors but not as controls that took over our ability to make decisions. Eventually we were all won over. "The extension of perception and the integration of the knowledge

Integration of energy and architecture with water-pumping windmill, solar water heater, dome, and reflective panels.

of cybernetics," we later explained, "will hopefully improve the way we think, and could be seen in this light as an exploratory survival skill." From then on, we came to view our computers as part of our transformative tool kit.

The Cape Cod Ark was completed by the summer of 1976. It was set low and snug amid the grasses and flowers of the field around it. This was partly because an earthen berm, piled high on the north wall for insulation, left only the roof visible from that side. From the south, the translucent fiberglass glazing, which made up the roof and much of that wall, was the material most in evidence. It was clear and whitish and shaped into a series of concave scallops. The roof and wall were configured to form a single, long-angled slope. Its steeped roofline was intended to reflect traditional Cape Cod architectural lines. Because the roof almost reached the top of the berm on the north side and the glazing extended almost to the ground for most of the south wall, the building appeared almost triangular. Partly reminiscent of other greenhouses, but with a local touch in its lines, the Ark was really without architectural precedent. Seen from a distance, it had something of the air of a boat, sails aslant, beached in a meadow.

The living world remained our conceptual model for the architecture of the bioshelters. Evolution is continuous, dynamic, and highly adaptive. As John was wont to point out, the Laws of Thermodynamics determine that there is progressive deterioration in the quality of energy, but living forms create spatial form and

The Cape Cod Ark,
as seen from slightly
northwest.

morphic order. In defiance of entropy, energy can be harnessed to work on the side
of life—which is precisely what we were trying to do. The Cape Cod Ark represented the miniaturization of an ecosystem. It was intended to be a microcosm
that absorbed and intensified the pulses of natural forces to provide an optimal
environment for life-forms ranging from soil animals to fish to people. The Ark
was our first exploration of the fruitfulness of a marriage between biology and
architecture.

The interior of the Ark consisted of a large central area that, in addition to the
ubiquitous plants, housed technical equipment and served as a small, open, meeting or teaching space. Opposite the front door was what looked like a concrete
bunker but in fact was a rock-filled heat storage area. Its upper surface area was
for experimental vine crops. In front of it was a sunken fish-culturing pond that
was also a source—again following in the steps of Beatrix Potter's Mr. McGregor—
of nutrient-enriched irrigation water. It was also home to a number of large and
splendid bullfrogs of the type that, in fairy tales, usually turn out to be princes in

a.

b.

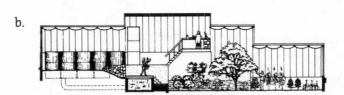

c.

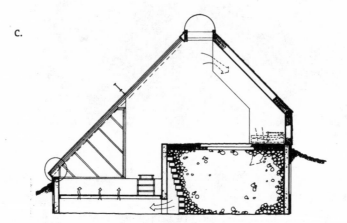

d.

(a) The Ark from the south side; (b) the Ark from the north side; (c) interior showing rock heat storage system; (d) interior showing solar-algae pond for aquaculture and heat storage.

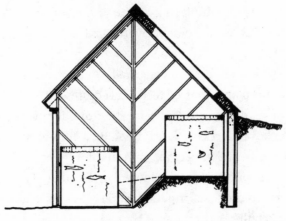

disguise. In the Ark they were the delight of visiting schoolchildren. A humidity-controlled, glass-fronted case behind the rock storage area housed a microcomputer. Suspended above all this, just below the pointed roof, was a small platform that served as a combination perch, observatory, and laboratory. The space around this heat storage area was designated to evaluate food crops suited to the Ark's solar climate.

The sun was to provide all the light and heating, but as a precautionary measure, we installed a wood-burning stove. It was never used, and we later removed it. Running along the south wall was a low bench to accommodate the propagation of tree, flower, and vegetable seedlings. The aquaculture facility, consisting of nine of the larger solar-algae ponds, occupied the west end of the Ark, with five additional tanks in the central agricultural zone. As we monitored the performance of the Ark in its early seasons, we discovered that providing a growing environment for fish was not to be the only contribution of the solar-algae ponds. The tanks were also proving to be excellent passive solar collectors. Ron Zweig's records and calculations indicated that during the unusually severe winter of 1977–78, the ponds inside the exclusively solar-heated Ark contributed the equivalent of approximately 2 gallons of heating oil a day at the going cost of a dollar a day. "The results," concluded Ron, "indicate a valuable secondary aspect of the aquaculture facility for the Ark." Eventually we dropped the rock storage unit in favor of increasing the number of tanks.

South face of the Ark in winter.

CAPE COD ARK

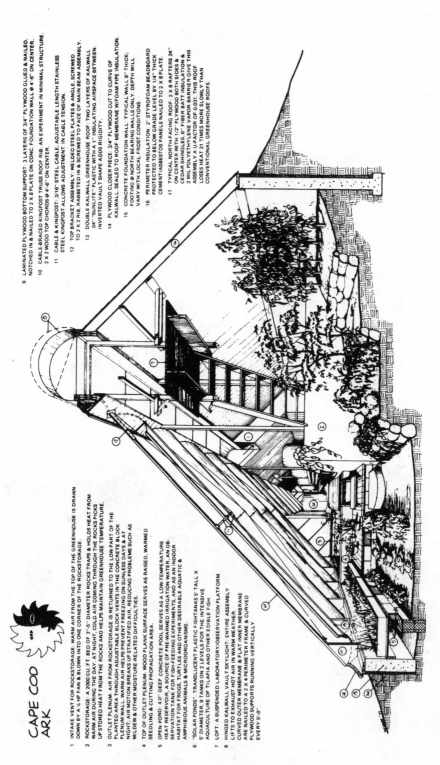

1. INTAKE VENT FOR ROCKSTORAGE. WARM AIR FROM THE TOP OF THE GREENHOUSE IS DRAWN DOWN BY A ⅓ HP FAN & BLOWN INTO ONE CORNER OF THE ROCKSTORAGE

2. ROCKSTORAGE: A 2000 CU. FT. BED OF 3"-5" DIAMETER ROCKS TRAPS & HOLDS HEAT FROM WARM AIR DURING THE DAY. AT NIGHT, COLD AIR COMING THROUGH THE ROCKS PICKS UP STORED HEAT FROM THE ROCKS AND HELPS MAINTAIN GREENHOUSE TEMPERATURE.

3. OUTLET PLENUM: AIR FROM ROCKSTORAGE IS RETURNED TO THE LOW PART OF THE PLANTED AREA THROUGH ADJUSTABLE BLOCK VENTS IN THE CONCRETE BLOCK PLENUM WALL. WARM AIR HELPS PREVENT FREEZING ON SUNLESS DAYS & AT NIGHT. AIR MOTION BREAKS UP STRATIFIED AIR, REDUCING PROBLEMS SUCH AS MILDEW & OTHER MOISTURE-RELATED DIFFICULTIES.

4. TOP OF OUTLET PLENUM: WOOD PLANK SURFACE SERVES AS RAISED, WARMED SEEDLING & CUTTING PROPAGATION AREA.

5. OPEN POND: 4.0' DEEP CONCRETE POOL SERVES AS A LOW-TEMPERATURE HEAT RESERVOIR, A SOURCE OF PRE-WARMED IRRIGATION WATER, AN OB-SERVATION TANK FOR FISH-FEEDING EXPERIMENTS, AND AS AN INDOOR HABITAT FOR FROGS, TURTLES AND OTHER DESIRABLE AQUATIC & AMPHIBIOUS ANIMALS & MICROORGANISMS.

6. "SOLAR PONDS": TRANSLUCENT PLASTIC FISHTANKS 5' TALL x 5' DIAMETER. 9 TANKS ON 2 LEVELS FOR THE INTENSIVE AQUACULTURE OF TILAPIA AND OTHER EDIBLE FISH.

7. LOFT: A SUSPENDED LABORATORY/OBSERVATION PLATFORM.

8. HINGED KALWALL VAULT SKYLIGHT: ENTIRE ASSEMBLY LIFTS TO EXHAUST HOT AIR IN WARM WEATHER. CURVED OUTER MEMBRANE & FLAT INNER MEMBRANE ARE NAILED TO A 2 X 4 PERIMETER FRAME & CURVED PLYWOOD SUPPORTS RUNNING VERTICALLY EVERY 5'-0".

9. LAMINATED PLYWOOD BOTTOM SUPPORT: 3 LAYERS OF 3/4" PLYWOOD GLUED & NAILED. NOTCHED IN & NAILED TO 2 X 8 PLATE ON CONC. FOUNDATION WALL @ 4'-6" ON CENTER.

10. CABLE-BRACED KINGPOST TRUSS ROOF RIB: AN EXPERIMENT IN MINIMAL STRUCTURE. 2 X 2 WOOD TOP CHORDS @ 4'-6" ON CENTER.

11. CABLE & KINGPOST: 3/16" STEEL CABLE. ADJUSTABLE LENGTH STAINLESS STEEL KINGPOST ALLOWS ADJUSTMENT IN CABLE TENSION.

12. TOP BRACKET ASSEMBLY: WELDED STEEL PLATES & ANGLE, SCREWED TO 2 X 2 RIB, RABBETED IN & SCREWED TO FACE OF MAIN BEAM ASSEMBLY.

13. DOUBLE KALWALL GREENHOUSE ROOF: TWO LAYERS OF KALWALL .04" "SUNLITE" PLASTIC WITH A 1" INSULATING AIRSPACE BETWEEN. INVERTED VAULT SHAPE ADDS RIGIDITY.

14. PLYWOOD CLOSER PIECE: 3/4" PLYWOOD CUT TO CURVE OF KALWALL. SEALED TO ROOF MEMBRANE W/FOAM PIPE INSULATION.

15. CONCRETE FOUNDATION WALL: TYPICAL WALL 8" THICK; FOOTING @ NORTH BEARING WALLS ONLY. DEPTH WILL VARY WITH LOCAL FROST CONDITIONS.

16. PERIMETER INSULATION 2" STYROFOAM BEADBOARD PROTECTED TO BELOW GRADE LEVEL BY 1/4" THICK CEMENT/ASBESTOS PANELS NAILED TO 2 X 8 PLATE.

17. TYPICAL NORTH-FACING ROOF: 2 X 8 RAFTERS 24" ON CENTER WITH 1/2" PLYWOOD BOTH SIDES & CEDAR SHINGLES. 6" FIBER BATT INSULATION & 2 MIL POLYETHYLENE VAPOR BARRIER GIVE THIS ASSEMBLY A U-FACTOR OF 0.031. THIS ROOF LOSES HEAT 21 TIMES MORE SLOWLY THAN CONVENTIONAL GREENHOUSE ROOFS.

Cross section of the Ark.

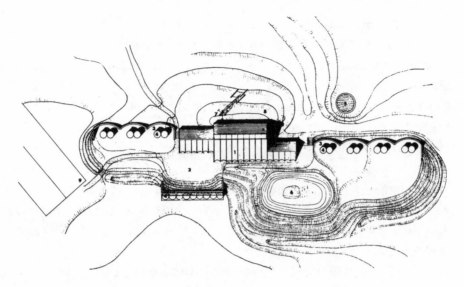

Overhead sketch of the Ark and solar courtyard.

Earle Barnhart explained the interconnections we were studying in the Arks: "The components of living systems have mechanisms of collection and storage to cope with fluctuations of energy supply. Plants generally absorb sunlight and store energy chemically as sugars, starches, or other materials in their structure. Many animals ingest food energy periodically but use it gradually. When plant and animal strategies co-evolve over time at the level of the ecosystem, a structure is developed that reduces the effects of extreme fluctuation of temperature, humidity, wind, and other environmental parameters. An important result of such an interacting community is a mutual reduction of physiological stress on its members."

Attempting to maximize productivity in the Arks and, as ever, drawing on observations of the natural world, we introduced a range of elements that would evolve and, in turn, nurture a diversity of plants and animals. Our goal was deep, biologically rich soils and organisms that would fill every available ecological niche and habitat. Our soil was not sterilized, as is standard greenhouse practice in order to guard against mold and plant disease. Nor could we resort to biocides, which would have been lethal to the fish. To assemble organisms adapted to a range of microclimates, we hauled in soils replete with bacteria and microorganisms from garden, field, meadow, and forest floor. We introduced further diversity with samples from alluvial, limestone, and glacial areas of southern New England. We also added liberal portions of compost, seaweed, and earthworms. In zones where light was limited, we gradually established small biological islands or refuge areas intended to harbor populations of predators, parasites, and pollinators the plants would need. Undisturbed by seasonal harvesting, these islands were pockets of herbs, flowers, grasses, meadow sod, or forest litter set in a rotting log, a section of stone wall, a tiny pond, or a permanent tree or vine.

A year or so after completion, the first major modification to the building was the addition of an exterior solar courtyard. It consisted of two thick walls, about 8 feet in height, one extending from the east and the other from the west end of the building. They were made of white concrete and scalloped to echo the shape of the glazing and to provide a series of shallow bays or apses. The walls served as shelter from all but south winds and acted as reflectors for the series of solar-algae ponds aligned in front of them. The entire ground area in front of the building was covered with white marble chips. This maximizing of light on sunny days created a dazzling brightness reminiscent of the whitewashed villages of the Mediterranean.

Management of the inside of the Ark fell to newcomers Kathi Ryan and Colleen Armstrong. They were a good team. Colleen had studied biology at the University of Michigan before migrating to Boston and then to the Cape, and she had a strong scientific bent. Kathi, a young friend who had been our babysitter in California, had a loving touch with plants, which thrived in her care. Their early research involved selecting and testing plants best suited to the interior climate of the bioshelter. The first winter they tested varieties of lettuce, kale, Swiss chard, spinach, parsley, endive, beet and turnip greens, and a selection of herbs. As the air and soil warmed with the spring, they planted melons, peppers, okra, and tomatoes. Later still, they installed a few tropical fruit trees.

Their summer research was mainly focused on pest control. Although there were few problems over the winter, by mid-April, like most other creatures, the pests revived and made their presence known. The predators in residence included spiders, lacewings, damselflies, praying mantises, predatory mites, chameleons, toads, frogs, and snakes. Colleen reported, "To the chagrin of the pests we too are a part of the Ark community and our role as pest managers must be as dynamic as that of the ecosystem. Our intrusions on its development are both physical and biological. We are engaged in the process of information gathering, monitoring numbers of insect pests, evaluating the agricultural environment, and finally deciding what actions to take." Kathi and Colleen were able to keep whiteflies under control with the wasp *Encarsia formosa*. As *Encarsia*, like tilapia, is native to the tropics, they were not expected to survive the winter. But prevail they did, and succeeding generations made the Ark their permanent home. In their battle against aphids, Kathi and Colleen incorporated a parasitic fungus, *Entomophthora*, and a parasitic insect, *Aphidius matricariae*, into their pest management regime as control agents. As insurance against red spider mites, they released another predatory mite, *Phytoseiulus persimilis*. Armed with such allies,

Horticulture section of the Ark.

and backed up by careful observation and vigilance, Kathi and Colleen were able to hold their own against pests.

Somehow the feel of the Ark was unlike that of any of its smaller predecessors. Our new bioshelter was much our largest so far at 90 feet in length, 30 in width, and stretching up to 25 in height at the peak of the roof. Whether it was a factor of size, or height, or mass, or just so much nature stuffed into a small space, it was a world unto itself and a lovely place to be. Particularly in winter or during spells of inclement weather, it was a haven for those of us who languished without our hands in dirt. I had a halcyon moment one February day while giving a tour to a small group of adults and children when the Ark was well past its solstice slump. There was a bitter wind, but bright sun was glancing off icy snow. The sensation on opening the door was like leaving winter behind and stepping out of a plane into the tropics. We were engulfed by moist, soft, warm air and the smells of plants and soil. The next impression was of green, of the depth and vibrancy of the greens of the plants in contrast to the hard, bright, white-and-blue reality on which we had just closed the door. Our first impulse was to strip off heavy jackets and hats. The children adapted immediately and dashed around discovering frogs and flowers and a strawberry just beginning to blossom. As I launched into an explanation of the building, we drifted about, enjoying the flowers: nasturtiums, geraniums, alyssum, and the inevitable New Alchemy marigolds. We examined the vegetables and herbs and wended our way to the solar-algae ponds

Interior of the Ark.

where the children promptly glued their noses to the outer wall of one of the tanks, waiting for fish to emerge from the gloom of dark, algae-laden water. Granted the odds in terms of timing and winter sun were in our favor that day, but selling the concept of the bioshelter was utterly redundant. The Ark spoke for itself.

Of course, as with all bioshelters, there were problems. Our prominent complaints about the Ark were inadequate ventilation; inefficient use of vertical space; lack of light on the north side; poor circulation of warmed air; use of wood in areas

Aquaculture section of the Ark as seen from the platform.

ECONOMIC
EVALUATION
DO NOT PICK
TOMATOES!

Organic tomatoes
ripening inside the Ark.

where dampness collected; poor drainage; and poor performance of the rock storage heat area in comparison to the solar-algae ponds. But we loved our newest bioshelter. It was a creative integrative statement that made a compelling case for passive solar heating and year-round gardening with potential for vast energy savings. It was a persuasive anti-nuclear statement. The Ark was a living laboratory—and a wonderful place to work. Robert Sardinsky found it a marvelous classroom for schoolchildren. In his words, "It's funky, alive, beautiful, and by golly, it works."

Our mixed reviews notwithstanding, in the late 1970s when New Alchemy was being assessed for the Rockefeller Brothers Fund, the scientific adviser, Dr. Barry Valentine, clearly got what we were trying to do. With a background in evolution, entomology, and tropical ecology, he had considered the bioshelter an interesting but probably unworkable idea. "I was wrong," he conceded. "It *is* working." His report continued: "The day of my visit was cold and overcast. On that day twenty persons were fed lunch from the Ark's vegetable garden, and all were invited to pick more. This garden is harvested daily so the produce was not an accumulation over time, but represented normal daily output. The garden was solid with vegetables and some flowers, productivity was high, and insect damage was minimal, mostly some leaf curling due to aphids that, in turn, were being attacked by parasitic wasps and fungi. As an entomologist, I was astonished at the very low level of insect damage."

The Bucky Dome

Several years after the Ark was fully operational, the innovative among us were leaning toward yet another new bioshelter project. This was the brainchild of J. Baldwin, the soft-technology editor of the Whole Earth publications who had recently come on board. He urged we attempt to synthesize our work with the architectural concepts of the maverick genius R. Buckminster Fuller, who had designed the first geodesic dome to follow the mathematics of Earth's great circle arcs. Monitoring the Ark had led Joe Seale and John Wolfe to do computer simulations on other configurations for bioshelters. The results made a strong case for having another go at a geodesic dome, better constructed than our earlier efforts. Although the Ark remained our flagship bioshelter, we were always interested in testing other models for improved levels of integration and productive capacity. To J.'s satisfaction we began work on the design of what was to be called the pillow dome. One of his goals was to avoid the corrosion and rot caused by condensation, to which our other bioshelters were prone. While hardly surprising considering the levels of humidity typical of greenhouses, it was a problem in search of cre-

ative solutions of the J. Baldwin variety. For ethical and environmental reasons he
rejected the possibility of constructing the frame with either rot-resistant redwood or other kinds of wood that had been treated with toxic preservatives. He
was also bent on producing an affordable building.

J. made the case for utilizing aluminum and plastic for the pillow dome. The
merits of his claims were made more persuasive by an accompanying photograph. Wearing his signature Peruvian cap, he was shown bouncing gleefully on
an inflated panel, grinning from ear to ear. "Aluminum is O.K.," he wrote. "It is a
high-energy material to make, but it does not disappear over time and can be recycled, often without reprocessing. It's readily available, not horribly expensive,
and lends itself well to mass production techniques." As for the glazing, he reasoned, "many folks, including me, like glass best. But it is heavy, requiring equally
heavy support, and it breaks. Most plastics are degraded by sunlight and damp
heat. Nonetheless, we have decided to do some experiments with the Du Pont Corporation's Teflon transparent films, which have great strength and longevity.
They are extraordinarily clear, have high transmisivity, and admit ultraviolet
wavelengths blocked by most glazing materials. I have had experience with inflated panels, which are stiff, tough, and easy to make. The pillows, inflated with
gas, will serve as insulation for the clear-sided dome. A logical way to utilize the
panels and the aluminum is in a geodesic dome frame. So here we go! Plans are
to make the inflated pillows from Tefzel and affix these panels to the dome frame
by means of clamping strips. The structure will give us valuable information on
the use of such materials as well as much data on the performance of domes."

John and newcomer/whiz kid John Wolfe did the legwork on researching and
acquiring the glazing from Du Pont. When energy expert Amory Lovins got wind
of the project, he suggested we use argon gas for inflating the panels. His reasoning was that argon is nontoxic and has superior insulating properties to air
because of its low thermal conductivity. Joe did the math on the relative insulating properties of gases. His results corroborated Amory's recommendation. A Massachusetts firm fabricated the pillows. In one way or another, most of the New
Alchemy staff were involved in the interior design and preparation of the 10,000-
square-foot growing space.

The top section of the dome had already been assembled and the triangles of
the lower half were in place when, one bright March morning, the time arrived
for the communal dome raising. Everyone abandoned their accustomed posts,
and a large cheerful crew gathered behind the farmhouse for the final assembly
of J.'s 30-foot-diameter dream dome. With the frame completed, the hazardous
transport of the fragile-looking, 500-pound bubble was next. Its intended home
overlooked the garden 200 feet away. Intern Scott Stokoe reported, "Nineteen

Solar courtyard with
solar-algae ponds.

people surrounded the dome top and lifted it to waist height. Tilting, rising, and lowering, it hovered, then glided across the ground."

I watched from a distance. It was a rather surreal spectacle. When the entourage encountered a dip in the ground, its human appendages disappeared and a large, shiny bubble appeared to be transporting itself purposefully, if a bit unsteadily, over the landscape. That it was being borne to the site of its predecessor was determined by neither sentiment nor tradition. The earlier dome had sheltered an espaliered fig tree, planted years before, so prolific that conservation of that tree alone was rationale for a protective structure. Scott's account concluded, "With one final lift the fig was cleared and, held aloft, the upper dome was connected to the lower base triangles. It stands now as a testimony to both the economy of thoughtful design and the power of thoughtful, committed people."

For J., Greg Watson, and many of the rest of us, the best was yet to come: Buckminster Fuller had agreed to be the guest of honor at the official opening. The des-

The Pillow "Bucky" Dome.

ignated date was in early June, which is usually lovely on the Cape as the freshness of spring drifts toward summer's lushness. But the deities of the skies decreed otherwise. The day began gray and overcast. As early afternoon and the appointed time approached, it began to rain unrelentingly. Our excitement, however, was as palpable as the wet grass underfoot. J.'s and Greg's feelings about having Bucky in our midst infected all of us. He was then ninety-two, but still brilliant. He did not disappoint us. The rain deterred no one. Guests of honor, New Alchemists and their friends, Du Pont representatives, Bucky aficionados, and the media were all there to record the visit of the great man. The *Falmouth Enterprise* reported, "It was a celebration from beginning to end. A celebration of life, of intellect, of hard hours of work paying off, of the beginning of a new technology."

"Mr. Fuller is walking slowly," the reporter continued, "head erect in the rain toward the dome. He leans heavily on his dark, round handled wooden cane, favoring his right side. 'She's beautiful,' he says looking at the dome. Reporters and photographers move like a wave in front of and behind him. New Alchemy administrators hover around him like protective parents. Unlike the press, they change places every so often, moving from back to front, front to back, so everyone has a turn at his side." Bucky continued carefully across the lawn toward the rim of the garden, then down the wooden entry ramp into dome.

By then the interior was a tropical island of moist fecundity, green and teeming with plant life. Fish swarmed in the clear-sided solar-algae ponds, and the sen-

Inside the Pillow Dome
with fig tree and with
visitors on their way in.

tinel fig was laden with ripening fruit. Bucky turned to John, his face as open and delighted as a child's. "It's magnificent!" he said. "It's what I've always wanted to see. My architecture combined with your biology. I think it's an extraordinary job you have done." John replied, "We wanted to transport the genetic genius of the tropics to northern climates. The only way to do it was to turn to your architecture." J. described the structure of the dome as being like a snowflake—as pure physics. Aquaculture apprentice Peter Burgoon called it ego-less architecture. Bucky congratulated the Du Pont representatives for their contribution to the work. "Corporations," he told them pointedly, "should stop focusing only on how to make money, and start making sense." He called the kind of work we were doing at New Alchemy "the hope of the world."

By the end of the afternoon Bucky was visibly tired. John and I helped J. and Greg steer him through his good-byes so they could drive him back to Boston. He died less than a year later. For Greg, J., and John that day had been another epiphany, the culmination of years of study, research, design, experimentation, and planning. If, like the great Gothic cathedrals, the dome was a humbler product of ego-less architecture, a twentieth-century expression of pure natural form, it now stood at New Alchemy, honoring the greater glory of the life processes of Earth. It stands there still.

The larger significance of our integrative work, which culminated in the bioshelters, was more than substantiated when we encountered a concept that came as an ultimate confirmation of our long-held belief that the natural world would prove the source of instructions for how we were to live. It was a theory that was to make a whole cloth of our understanding of ecology. The Gaia Hypothesis, now advanced to the level of theory, was the brainchild of the British atmospheric chemist James Lovelock and the American microbiologist Lynn Margulis. First introduced by Dr. Lovelock in 1972 in the journal *Atmospheric Environment*, it was named for the Greek goddess of the earth.

The theory contends that Earth, as a planet, constitutes a single biogeophysical system—Dr. Lovelock called it a "living entity"—made up of countless interconnected, interdependent, self-organizing living systems and subsystems. The planet and its life-forms evolved as a unit, and the myriad life-forms on Earth are inseparable components of the planet itself. The theory, now generally termed Earth System Science, is now accepted in the mainstream scientific community worldwide. Gaia theory, in the words of Dr. Lovelock, "is a new way of organizing facts about life on Earth. It is a new view because it includes the evolution of the planet as well as that of the organisms upon it and it sees these hitherto separate evolutions as a single tightly coupled process." Elsewhere he explained, "The entire range of living matter on Earth from whales to viruses and from oaks to algae could be regarded as constituting a single living entity capable of maintaining the Earth's atmosphere to suit its overall needs and endowed with faculties and powers far beyond those of its constituent parts."

The evidence for life interacting at once on a planetary and a cellular scale was undreamed scientific affirmation of New Alchemy's ideas: an umbrella theory. Gaia described the processes and dynamics with which we were working on a much smaller scale in our semicontained ecosystems of ponds, gardens, and bioshelters. As John had written in the *Journal*: "The same forces that have shaped us have shaped the world. There can be no real separation. The continuities between the design of cells and ecosystems extend from organelles outward to the smallest fresh water pools, with their myriad living entities, to the oceans, and ultimately to the whole planet."

Through Gaia theory all life is connected. And New Alchemy, we came to realize, was a laboratory of applied Gaia.

chapter seven

An Ark for Prince Edward Island: A Live-in Bioshelter

> I like to think that the experience of the Ark and all those
> connected to it will be at the birth of the new philosophy,
> which we will then be able to call a technology.
> —Pierre Elliott Trudeau

Nineteen seventy-six was a pivotal year in the unfolding of New Alchemy. It not only marked the completion of the Cape Cod Ark, the culmination of our efforts in integration up until that time, but it also brought the parallel and simultaneous designing and building of a second Ark on Prince Edward Island in Canada. At times we felt sorely challenged. Not even the biblical Noah had attempted two Arks at once, and he had had fairly solid backing.

The idea of working in the Canadian Maritimes had almost as much magnetism for John Todd as did the Costa Rican center for Bill McLarney. On a trip to Ottawa John had met Andrew Wells, who was on the staff of Alex Campbell, the premier of Prince Edward Island, Canada's smallest province. Andrew Wells proved sympathetic to many of John's ideas. With strong contacts in both the federal and the provincial governments, Wells was able to open the right doors. As a result, in November 1974 Canada's Ministry of State for Urban Affairs, inspired by a recent conference on Habitat for Humanity, asked New Alchemy to conceptualize and design a structure for their United Nations Urban Demonstration Human Settlements Program.

We proposed to build a bioshelter that would integrate food growing, energy independence, research areas, waste treatment, and living quarters. David Bergmark and Ole Hammarlund, the architects for the

Cape Cod Ark, introduced their project in the *Journal*: "Integral to the design of the Prince Edward Island Ark was the incorporation of a residence, an extensive greenhouse area and seven hundred and fifty square feet of hot water solar collectors—all competing for a place in the sun." The Ark was to be an autonomous structure. It had to be able to withstand the rigorous Canadian winter. We wanted to create a building that was the antithesis of the standard North American dwelling that draws heavily on power grids and pollutes adjacent air, land, and water bodies with its wastes.

Once completed, the Ark was not to impinge heavily on the external world or pollute neighboring ecosystems or consume fossil fuel or nuclear power. It was to be a prototype of a building as a resource, producing food, plants, trees, and energy for the area around Spry Point. The Minister of Urban Affairs approved our proposal in January 1975, but it was another half year before we received the contract. We broke ground in October and immediately began construction of the Ark.

The Prince Edward Island chapter of our history, spanning a much shorter time than the near twenty year life of the Institute, seems somehow framed—a play within a play, a dream within a dream—encapsulating the pith of our history. Like New Alchemy, it was the story of an idea that was both of and ahead of its time. As we had come to realize from working on the Cape Cod Ark, the transformation from idea to actuality took prodigious effort. New Alchemy's Solsearch partners, David Bergmark and Ole Hammarlund, were not only our architects for both Arks, but they were our chief builders. Dividing their time between construction sites on the Cape and Prince Edward Island (PEI), they were working in constant overdrive. Nancy Willis, who was overseeing the installation of the biological systems in Canada throughout the winter, went with David. Ole moved back and forth between the island and the Cape. They had just enough of the framing up before the snow flew to tack up protective plastic for shelter and keep going. By spring, the building had taken shape. In May 1976 it passed government inspection. Then John, Bob Angevine, Ty Cashman, and Al Doolittle (who discovered that he could make the drive between the two Arks in the length of time it took him to play thirteen audiocassettes) also became commuters.

The natural setting of the Ark on the island's Spry Point was dramatically beautiful: a windblown promontory jutting into the Gulf of St. Lawrence. It was remote and surrounded by the sea on three sides. The coastline alternated between wide beaches and red sandstone cliffs. Open land stretched back from the shore to second- and third-growth forests. The area was wilder than the landscape of the rest of the island, which was mainly agricultural. There were few other buildings in sight. From the land side the Ark stood alone, a beacon at the tip of the peninsula.

Schematic overview of the
Prince Edward Island Ark
from the southwest.

Ambitious as the scope of the Cape Ark was as an integrated, food-growing, solar bioshelter, that of the Prince Edward Ark was more so. From the north side the Ark resembled an architecturally conservative contemporary house. Like its Cape counterpart, its visual impact was minimized by an earthen berm, which partially masked its size. The south side was almost industrial looking with its expanse of solar collectors, greenhouse glazing, and air ducts. To maximize the collecting surface, the topmost solar collector rose straight upward, billboard fashion, along the entire south façade. This also prevented snow buildup. This layer of collectors heated water for storage and for space heating the living quarters. The heated water was stored in a 20,000-gallon containment tank located below the residential area. A second, slanted row of collectors just below the vertical layer heated water for household use. Exposed ducts on both sides of the living area circulated the warmed air downward to a rock storage area. Our architects wrote that, from the west side, "the house took on a more inviting scale. There was a spectacular view of the sea and the afternoon sun was let freely into the living room, dining area, and bedrooms."

(top) The south face of the Prince Edward Island Ark; (bottom) the Island Ark from the northeast.

The Island Ark from the southeast.

The horticulture section of the greenhouse, like the Cape Ark, contained a rock heat-storage chamber as well as the water containment tank. The overall growing area was divided into two parts. The larger area was for experimenting with commercial crops; the smaller one, adjacent to the kitchen, was for growing food for the residents of the building. While food autonomy was not one of the design goals, the Island Ark was intended to produce fresh foods on a year-round basis. Over time we cultured an array of vegetables, herbs, and greens as well as fish. Flowers and young trees became equally important. The aquaculture facility was both solar collector and fish-culturing complex. It housed thirty-two linked solar-algae ponds. The tanks with their thriving algae populations, like those on the Cape, proved to be efficient collectors and stores of solar energy.

We designed the living space to look traditional and welcoming. The living room had pine wainscoting and a wood-burning stove for creature comfort and gave a protected feeling amid the vastness of sea and sky beyond the windows. Much of the furniture was built-in. Many of the added touches and books came from our own households; Susan Ervin's weavings, a series of nautical lithographs from John's parents, and a few cushions and rugs that we could spare from our households. Overall the effect was thoroughly pleasant; more homey than "house beautiful." And, although homey, it was not exactly ordinary. All household

The living room in the Island Ark.

The west end of the
Island Ark.

wastes were treated internally. This called for the installation of a composting toilet that also processed kitchen wastes. Our intention was to reduce water use, circumvent the need for sewage and sludge treatment, and produce fertilizer suitable for compost.

The Prince Edward Island Ark was our most advanced experiment in applying ecologically derived principles of design to human problems. In both residence and microfarm we had substituted sunlight and solar energy for fossil fuels. Drawing on the dynamics of natural ecosystems, we had also incorporated elements of advanced integration, redundancy, diversity, renewable energy sources, photosynthetically based food chains, microbial pathways for self-regulation, internal homeostasis, and mutually beneficial interphasing with adjacent ecosystems. In the *CoEvolution Quarterly* for summer 1976, John summarized the scientific guidelines for sustainability set forth by New Alchemy, which we hoped the Ark would manifest:

1. Engage in design and research on a micro level while maintaining a planetary perspective and a concern between levels of organization.
2. Emphasize food-producing and energy systems that do not require large amounts of capital.
3. Seek methods by which a gradual shift could be made from a hardware-intensive society to an informationally and biologically extensive one.
4. Emphasize participatory solutions, which could involve large segments of society.
5. Explore bioregional approaches to the future.
6. Seek methods for incorporating renewable energy sources and durable materials in lieu of finite substances.

To achieve the level of energy autonomy we had in mind for the Ark, an electricity-generating windmill seemed a natural. Prince Edward Island was ideally suited as a testing ground for wind power. The island has an excellent wind profile, and Spry Point, being remote and primarily rural, did not have a high per capita energy demand. In addition, we knew that Prince Edward Island, with the neighboring province of New Brunswick, was considering a nuclear future. We hoped that an efficient, economic demonstration windmill on the Ark site might affect future energy decisions in the province and beyond. To offset our admittedly slim qualifications to design such a system, we turned to professional consulting engineers Merrill Hall and Vince Dempsey to head the project. Among the New Alchemists, Bob Angevine, who as a colonel in the Signal Corps had designed a military communications in Vietnam, was an obvious asset. Ty Cashman, who

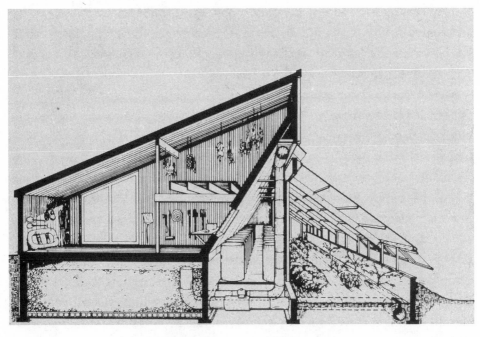

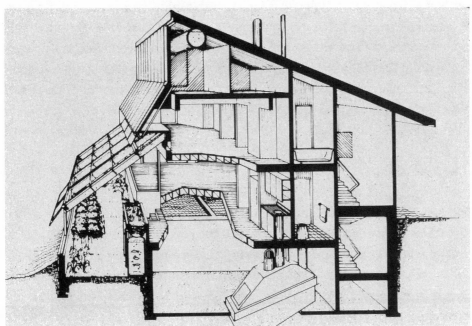

(top) Cross section of the Island Ark from the east; (bottom) cross section of the Island Ark's living quarters.

was increasingly grounding his philosophic background with hands-on skills, also signed on with the windmill crew. Later, feeling we still lacked the sufficient knowledge of physics to link the energy and engineering systems, Ty brought on physicist Joe Seale to complete the team.

Merrill and Vince conceived and designed an experimental windmill that came to be called the Hydrowind. The Hydrowind was to be powerful enough to provide the overall power needs for the Ark or for a large farm. It was a 25-kilowatt, horizontal-axis wind turbine that used hydraulic fluids to transfer energy from the blades to the generating station at the foot of the tower. An innovative feature of the Hydrowind was the dual, lightweight blades, which were based on an internal tension system. According to Joe Seale, equally innovative was "the use of a hydraulic pump at the top of the forty foot tower to receive power from the rotor and deliver it in the form of pressurized hydraulic flow to ground-based equipment. To generate electricity a hydraulic motor, driven by the flow of fluid from the top of the mill, turned a permanent field, brushless electric generator. The alternating current from the generator varied in both voltage and frequency with wind speed changes and was incompatible with fixed voltage utility lines. To overcome this, an electronic synchronous inverter transformed the wind-generated electricity to the proper voltage and frequency and combined it with electricity from the utility." When electricity generated by the Hydrowind exceeded the Ark's consumption, the surplus power was to be sent into the Island's grid through the utility lines.

The Countdown

Whereas the deadline for completion of the Ark on the Cape had not been cast in stone, it was on Prince Edward Island, and the pressure was acute. Both federal and provincial governments were keeping a close eye on the Ark's progress. And, not only that, it was rumored that Canadian Prime Minister Pierre Elliott Trudeau might be interested in officiating at the opening ceremony. This was an unprecedented honor. The dashing Mr. Trudeau was a celebrity, a leader on the world stage, and one of Canada's greatest statesmen. With the likelihood of his attending, the opening date of September 22, 1976, became nonnegotiable.

As that summer came on, the pace at Spry Point picked up. It was made no less frantic by the unending stream of visitors, authorized and otherwise. The innate courtesy and good humor of Nancy and David, who managed to receive visitors with trowel or hammer in hand, was a main factor in keeping things moving forward. Although the rate of commuting between the two New Alchemy centers had been on the rise all summer, a serious influx of help in terms of numbers did not really begin until the first week of September. From then on until opening day not only the numbers of people but the intensity and focus of their efforts were remarkable. Toward the end many of us were working twenty-hour days and subsisting largely on caffeine. There were periods when David and Ole rarely slept at all. Most of the time it seemed preposterous that we should ever be ready on time.

As it was so often at New Alchemy gatherings, the people who arrived, for whatever reasons, were varied and wonderful. Many of the long-haired young appeared, of course, arriving in vans or on foot with packsacks. Some of them wanted to settle in and really work; they stayed and proved invaluable. Others watched for a while then drifted away. Old friends also kept arriving, as did neighbors from the Woods Hole community, summer people, relatives, families, and longtime fellow travelers such as *Whole Earth* publications veterans J. Baldwin and Kathl Whitacre. Academics wielded hammers and paintbrushes beside poets, plumbers, and homesteaders. People from the local community gave up their Sundays to stay on the job.

With the days until the deadline dwindling to less than a week, the intensity increased exponentially. In ways it was the closest experience any of us are likely to have to participating in an ant colony. Definite patterns began to emerge. People were greeted exuberantly on arrival. They would spend an hour or so looking around, then were absorbed into the dynamic, becoming contributing members of the humming, ordered pattern, the organization of which was not discernible to the casual eye. It was not uncommon to see any undone but essential task undertaken, carried out, and completed almost as one watched, rather like time-lapse photography. Forty-eight hours before the opening, for example, beyond an earlier seeding of grass that was just beginning to germinate, virtually no landscaping had been done. The building itself was surrounded by rutted mud. Then, in almost no time, the front walk was graveled and smoothed; shrubs were dug up from the fields and transplanted; rocks were hauled from the beach for walkways; paths were laid out and lined with stones; a seaweed mulch was spread over the exposed ground. Industrious lines of people raked or trekked seaweed or lugged rocks. Another crew painted window frames and vent hatches. The biologists and their assistants worked with the solar-algae ponds, fending off enthusiastic children who had slightly different ideas about the purpose and flow of the aquatic systems. The only major failing in managing such a goal-oriented yet ad hoc operation was that we had made no collective provision for food, leaving individuals or groups to fend for themselves. People often worked until they were exhausted before they took a break to eat. Too late we realized we easily could have organized a food crew, and we vowed never to let such a lapse occur again.

The Hydrowind.

With the help of a crane—borrowed from an assignment on a nearby church steeple—the Hydrowind was up and affixed to its tower. But, frustratingly, it was not starting in the strong wind, and there was a lot of speculation as to why. The windmill crew spent long hours being buffeted on the tower while making adjustments. The consensus was that in attempting to avoid mishaps, they had set the blade angle too conservatively. J. Baldwin reported on the project in the winter 1976–77 issue of the *CoEvolution Quarterly*. He noted John saying, "I want that thing roaring for Trudeau." His account continued: "The days and nights have melted together. Many more Alchemists and friends have appeared and are put to work. Premier Alex Campbell comes by to make sure that all will be in readiness and not an embarrassment. He accepts John's assurances but you can tell he's not sure. The entire Ark and surrounding area is getting worse looking by the hour. Huge piles of junk appear as the interior is being finished up. I see a woman with yellow blotches on the seat of her pants and I know that somewhere there is a closet door that will have to be retouched."

In spite of sporadic meals, as the hours ticked by, one by one, the jobs were completed. Complicated ones, such as installing the sprinkling system in the greenhouse, which had kept J. and Kathl aloft on the scaffolding for several days, were eventually finished. So were the more domestic ones, such as sanding and polishing the living room floor, which was done between one and four on the morning of the fateful day by Michaela Walsh, a supporter from the Rockefeller Brothers Fund, along with Ole and myself, and a large, bearded fellow whom I never saw again. By ten o'clock on the morning of the opening, the living quarters were declared ready for finishing touches, and I had the fun of setting out flowers and hanging paintings. In the same final hours, the Hydrowind crew was still fine-tuning. Then, with Al Doolittle monitoring the controls, in a final burst of glory—or effort—Ty and Vince threw the switch and the Hydrowind pumped electricity into the Island's grid for the first time.

Prime Minister Trudeau's arrival had been scheduled for one thirty that afternoon. At twelve thirty we scattered to change. In addition to inadequate food arrangements, there were virtually no washing facilities for the group, which now amounted to more than a hundred. Most of us had been living in tents or vans for weeks and were thoroughly coated in paint, dirt, fire smoke, grease, or a combination of these. The nearest available showers were at the provincial campgrounds. Those of us who did not descend on Nancy Willis's household gathered up kids and went off to wash there. With such token grooming we did our best to appear civilized, and it probably wasn't the first time Mr. Trudeau had been greeted by people with paint-encrusted fingernails. Most of us were careful not to display our hands, and if he noticed turpentine to be the predominant perfume, he was too polite to comment.

According to J., "We split to our tent to clean up a little. When we return the Ark looks like something from another planet. Spotless! Fresh flowers everywhere inside. Fresh fruit. John and his crew have planted trees all over the place! Some crew has laid out hundreds of feet of neat gravel paths. The whole place glitters in the sun, a beautiful day in the midst of a rainy season. A fresh wind comes up and the Hydrowind whizzes, actually making power for the first time."

The Ark Achieves Its Moment in Time

And so it was that, more or less ready, more or less dressed, somewhat cleaner than we had been in some time, with the Ark functional and gleaming, the lot of us—New Alchemists and friends in the company of several hundred islanders and the inevitable swarm of media—were clustered and gazing skyward when the helicopters bearing Mr. Trudeau and Premier Alex Campbell and his wife ap-

The Todds flanked by Premier Campbell (left) and Prime Minister Trudeau. *Second row, left to right,* Dorothy Todd Henaut, Nancy Bodkin, Rebecca Todd, and Susannah Todd.

peared in the sky. The children shrieked and surged with excitement in the tornado of the landing. The dignitaries disembarked and were greeted, then made their way through the throng and across the field to mount the deck at the west end of the Ark. J. Baldwin noted, "No cops or secret service at all! Not a gun in sight!"

The opening ceremonies began. Mr. Trudeau, Mr. Campbell, and John spoke briefly and appropriately on the meaning of the occasion. It was clear that Mr. Trudeau understood the implications of what we were trying to do. He read aloud John's words on the plaque that dedicated the building:

> The Ark
> An Early Exploration
> In Weaving Together
> The Sun, Wind, Biology,
> And Architecture
> On Behalf of Humanity.

Then he went on to address the crowd: "Those who are concerned about the future of mankind [*sic*] are haunted by three questions: will there be enough food, will we have enough energy, and can we produce both without destroying the environment? The Ark—which I have the pleasure of declaring officially open today—the Ark is answering 'Yes!' to those three questions. And that is why I consider it a very exciting moment."

Prime Minister Pierre Trudeau addressing the crowd at the opening.

"The high mechanistic civilization, which we have developed," he continued, "has produced great abundance, great affluence, but it is also destroying the Earth. All the wonderful machines we have created are the great creations of the human brain. But we have not yet built a philosophy of those machines. And this is what is being done here in a practical way. I like to think that the experience of the Ark and all those connected to it will be at the birth of the new philosophy, which we will be able then to call a technology." So saying, Prime Minister Trudeau defined the Ark at its moment in time. Our Canadian bioshelter had become a reality.

Once the formalities were over, John and I gave Mr. Trudeau and the Campbells a tour with a fairly detailed explanation of the Ark and its workings. John guided them through the horticulture/aquaculture area, describing the potential of the year-round culture of food for a northern climate. He pointed out the heat storage areas and discussed the energetics of the building. Then we climbed the stairs from the greenhouse to the living area, newly finished and shining, and ended by admiring the view of the sea from the living room windows. When John had finished, Mr. Trudeau told us that he would like to have a similar house for his family.

A comparison of the Ark with orthodox housing.

Category	Ark	Orthodox Housing
UTILIZES THE SUN	Source of heating, climate, purification, food production, and much interior light.	Some interior light—often negative role necessitating air conditioning.
UTILIZES THE WIND	A source of electrical energy from windmill wind-driven circulation through composting toilet.	Only negatively, increasing fuel demands through infiltration.
STORES ENERGY	Yes—in three systems and growing areas.	No.
MICRO-CLIMATOLOGICAL SITING	Integral to design.	Rare.
WASTE PURIFICATION	Yes—except for gray water, which is piped into leaching bed.	Wastes untreated and discharged to pollute.
WASTE UTILIZATION	Purified wastes are nutrient sources in interior biological cycles.	No.
FUEL USE	Wood, a renewable source, as supplemental heat.	Heavy use of gas, oil, or inefficient electricity.
ENERGY CONSERVING	Yes—also uses energy to serve simultaneous functions.	No, or rarely.
ELECTRICITY CONSUMPTION	About same as an orthodox house but electricity used for many productive and economic functions.	Fairly heavy consumer.
FOODS	Diverse foods cultured year-round.	Not within—often summer gardens.
AGRICULTURAL CROPS	Vegetables, flowers, and young trees.	No.
AQUACULTURAL PRODUCE	Fish for market.	No.
ECONOMIC UNIT	Yes—viability to be determined.	No—financial burden.
OPERATIONAL COST	Low—ultimately exporter or power.	High—particularly in fuels and electricity.
INITIAL COST	High—due to energy and biological components—uses larger amounts of quality materials.	Moderate.
VULNERABILITY TO INFLATION AND SHORTAGES	Slight.	Severe.
IMPROVES CLIMATE AND LOCAL ENVIRONMENT	Yes—locally by windbreak and more broadly through reforestation.	Rarely—most intensify weather.
TEACHES ABOUT THE LARGER WORKINGS OF NATURE	Yes.	No.
INCREASES SELF-SUFFICIENCY	Yes.	Rarely.
STIMULATES LOCAL AND REGIONAL SOLUTIONS	Possible.	Unlikely.

Having made a vow to myself, I seized the moment to tell Mr. Trudeau that the Ark was standing testimony to the fact that nuclear power was unnecessary and that New Alchemy was unalterably opposed to its development. Nuclear power was, I insisted, again quoting Princeton nuclear scientist Ted Taylor, based upon human and technological infallibility. Mr. Trudeau's response was polite but non-committal, which I accepted because I knew that he was a staunch advocate of nuclear disarmament in the international arena and I felt that he appreciated my concern even though he refrained from commenting.

There was not enough space for everyone to squeeze into the Ark during the official tour. Nancy Willis had foreseen this potential awkwardness and had gratefully accepted the offers of some of our Spry Point neighbors to set up a tent and bring refreshments. They produced literally thousands of sandwiches—all the more welcome for the recent dearth of food among us. Our neighbors were anxious that "the reception speak well of the people of Spry Point." Nancy obligingly invited some local musicians to come and play for everyone. There were to be two performances, one during the afternoon ceremony and another at an evening celebration. Without any insult intended to Mr. Trudeau and his party, it was quite clear to the rest of us which of the two performances the singer and star of the show considered more important. She had confided to some of us the night before that she couldn't count on her hair staying just right for both events. Reluctantly, saving herself for what she considered the really grand occasion, she performed that afternoon in her curlers.

Mr. Trudeau maintained his discretion and was appropriately appreciative. After the tour and the music, he and the Campbells snacked and chatted with the Islanders who had come to see them. Then their aides whisked them away into the sky again. William Irwin Thompson later maintained that, in opening the Ark personally and thereby acknowledging the possibility of an alternative course for the future, Mr. Trudeau had performed the most significant act by a major political figure for that decade. In a subsequent interview Prime Minister Trudeau named New Alchemy's work as embodying his hope for the future. He commented on the promise inherent in "realizing and strengthening the bonds among ourselves and between us and nature, toward stewardship of the Earth rather than exploitation and trusteeship rather than ownership."

The opening celebrations did not end with the departure of the helicopters. That night, with our Island neighbors and the visiting work crew, we had a gala party. Our neighbors once again provided the music, and everyone danced with everyone—kids and government officials, hippies and farmers and professors—all jounced around the packed living room until after midnight. Such was the height of the cheerful bedlam inside the Ark that in order to carry on a conversation, one had to either shout or retire to a point at some distance outside. J. Baldwin wrote, "Everyone is exhausted, proud, and happy and there is a good feeling in the air. The local people refer to the project as 'our Ark.' We've never seen anything like this." Stewart Brand summarized, "I'm not sure this needs to be said, but the opening of the Ark was in fact a moving—even triumphant—occasion. Such events usually aren't. This was. Like fiddle music for dancing."

Consecration of the House

We had one more event planned to round out the opening ceremonies, one that for me was among the most important. The next morning was to be the autumn equinox, and we had wanted to hold a silent sunrise vigil. But dawn brought the

The horticulture section of the Ark.

rain that had miraculously been held at bay all the preceding day. It drummed on the roofs of the vans and slid in sheets down the sides of our tents. It was cold and wet and dismal, and most of us, even the kids, were too tired to move. Instead, we rested in our sleeping bags a bit longer before gathering for one more time to restore the Ark from the ravages of the previous night. When that was done, we turned to mystic David Spangler, whom I had invited to join us to talk of the meaning of the Ark in its most profound sense. We sat in a circle around him in the living room while he spoke of what we hoped the Ark and ideas like it might come to mean—of the dream of a renewed understanding of the larger patterns of life and of the human place within those universal patterns.

Later, in his book *Emergence,* David wrote, "At one point during the celebrations I walked out to the cliff by myself and looked back. The entire south face of the Ark was covered in glass and solar panels. As I stood there, it caught the light of the sun and sky and was simply transformed into a building of light. It became ethereal, a temple of fire from some other dimensions, momentarily descended to Earth. The Ark seemed to be the outpost of a true planetary culture. A bioshelter is a mythic construct as well as a practical, ecological one. It is a portal into the mind of Gaia, a rite of identification with the processes of Earth, a symbol of how we may learn to think, not just about a planet, but as a planet. It is part of the knowledge we need in order to incarnate the planetary culture that is Gaia."

Amory Lovins subsequently wrote: "The biologically sophisticated Ark makes manifest our interdependence with the natural world, reintegrating us into it and enhancing our sense of wholeness: a special strength of combined innovation in energy and agricultural systems."

With David Spangler's words our house was consecrated and the opening ceremony complete. People began to pack, break camp, and depart rather quietly, leaving Nancy in charge of the Ark's overall operation and David and Ole to fine-tune a few last details. I don't think any of us have since experienced a time quite like those last few days, either in the intensity of the preparations or in the headiness of celebrations.

For New Alchemy, the opening of the Arks rounded out 1976 as a year of affirmation. We had proved, albeit on a small scale, that sustainable, ecologically sound analogues to the industrial paradigm were feasible and doable. We had learned what we sought when we started New Alchemy: "By turning to nature for guidance we hope, like karma yogis, to become attuned to the laws of nature through the practice that is our work." A number of authoritative minds agreed. René Dubos, the microbiologist whose research had led to the discovery of penicillin, wrote that our bioshelters "appear to me as arches linking the creative forces of nature with the control made possible by sophisticated technology."

chapter eight

A Period of Consolidation

The great revelation perhaps never did come.
Instead there were little daily miracles, illuminations,
matches struck unexpectedly in the dark.
—Virginia Woolf, *To the Lighthouse*

The years that followed the opening of the Ark on Prince Edward Island continued to substantiate our belief that New Alchemy was truly incubating the healing science we had sought from the beginning. Our soil grew ever more fertile, and our gardens were productive beyond expectation. The fish-raising programs continued to be innovative and successful. Our various windmills and bioshelters were making our systems more energy efficient and independent of the grid, standing as simple but cheerful prototypes of the viability of renewables and conservation. We were amassing sufficient evidence to believe that the question of providing for people while protecting and enhancing the environment could be answered in the affirmative, that humanity could—and still can—live sustainably on the planet. Our conviction was reinforced in 1978 when John and I were chosen as recipients of the Threshold Award. The award, which subsequently came to be referred to as an alternative Nobel Prize, honored "significant contributions to human knowledge in areas linking scientific, aesthetic, and religious ideas." We chose to see it as an affirmation of all New Alchemy had worked for.

Our confidence in our mission had also been corroborated publicly back in August 1976 when we again made the *New York Times*, this time as the cover story for the magazine section. There we were, about a dozen New Alchemists peering earnestly into one of the larger solar-algae ponds. The accompanying article by Wade Greene was aptly entitled, "The New Alchemists: Cooking Up a Gentle Science for Survival." The photo was obviously posed. That many people were not likely to be clustered around a tank at one time, and there was not much to see in its murky depths. But that level of coverage was clearly getting the message out, and we were glad to take time off and go along with the *Times* photographer as he shot us clambering on windmill towers and teetering on the edges of ponds.

Wade Greene, who wrote regularly on social and environmental issues for the *Times*, reported, "The paired high-voltage poles stand stiffly all along the gentle Pleistocene hills of south Cape Cod, bearing one hundred and fifteen thousand volts in their stunted arms. At one point along their route, where a dairy farm once operated, nestles a cluster of odd little wood and fiberglass structures; a windmill with red sails turns languidly in the breeze near a neatly tended garden patch. It is a pleasant, tinkertoy community. The electric transmission poles and the community in their shadow could hardly be more opposite. The cluster beneath the poles is a forward camp in a movement to achieve smallness and innocuousness in our technology, ultimately in our way of life itself. . . . The New Alchemists, probably more than any other group, have brought a high degree of expertise, organization and implementation to their quest, and, in the process, they have accumulated a respectable following for both their visionary and their down-to-Earth means. " He concluded, "Generally speaking, the New Alchemists see their own horizons as limitless. They feel that they are pioneers in an area that has been barely explored and compare their potential to that of the Model T at the advent of the automobile age." He reported that I had pointed out, "If we're wrong, unlike nuclear technologies, we really haven't hurt anybody." And if we were right? Wade Greene concluded, "the Alchemists will be the teachers of all of us."

At the end of our first decade, still believing that we had barely scratched the surface of its potential, New Alchemy crossed the threshold into the 1980s. Although we did not at the time see the writing on the wall, the Institute, too, was on the threshold of major changes. For one, I decided to resign from the staff and to devote myself to freelance writing and take more time to myself. New Alchemy was still, of course, very much part of me, and I still spent quite a bit of time out at the Farm to be with my friends and to help in the gardens. I remained on the board until the end.

John, too, was becoming involved in outside projects that were drawing him away more of the time. This led eventually to the founding of a second research institute, Ocean Arks International. Pondering his future course, he was watching Gary Hirshberg closely. Gary was then the youngest person on the staff, but his gift for leadership was unarguable. He didn't necessarily think along the group/party line, but any differences lay in strategy, not in vision or mission. He was articulate, had an engaging public manner, and showed an aptitude for fundraising. In the fall of 1980 John announced he planned to step aside and recommended Gary as his successor. The group agreed, and Gary became New Alchemy's second executive director.

That November brought Ronald Reagan's election as president as well as a Republican majority to Congress, an event that had repercussions far beyond our small world. It signaled the coming direction of government funding—or lack of it—and it was soon clear that New Alchemy would have to find ways of adapting to changing times. In the culture at large, the idealism that had fueled much of the work of the 1970s was losing ground to a focus on financial gain that was judged the criterion for legitimacy. Gary, for one, saw that programs such as that of our National Science Foundation team could not anticipate indefinite federal support. His was a more aikido-like approach to political and economic issues than that of some of the older Alchemists. Whereas we had always been inclined to joust full tilt at ideas with which we disagreed, Gary stood back to analyze a given dynamic and assess where our strengths might be most effectively placed.

Some of us thought it was not our role to justify New Alchemy's work in terms of the marketplace. Others argued that this might be the most effective strategy in the long run. It was becoming obvious that we would either have to raise money from the private sector or generate it ourselves. Some of our group meetings took directions that would have been unheard of in earlier years. Whereas self-doubt had never visited any of us then, with the greater financial uncertainty some of us began to doubt the feasibility of our mission. Even the founding vision we worked so long to articulate and implement was called into question. How to remain leading edge in the field of ecological thinking and design, which was the reason for our existence, while streamlining the Institute to become more professional, efficient, and saleable? At times the combination of new people and new thinking made it harder to operate within the informal and flexible structure that had served us for so long. Like a family, we had operated on many unspoken and unwritten assumptions, all of us trusting that each of us would honor our commitment in our own way. This was becoming harder to sustain. After one wearying round of discussions, Ron Zweig summed up our decision-making process as "consensus through exhaustion."

Gary outlined our predicament as follows: "Our work at New Alchemy is based on an ecological paradigm. That is why our theory of design places a greater emphasis on cyclical, biological principles than it does on fixed, physical laws. Since traditional economics is, for the most part, derived from a classical Newtonian mechanistic worldview, it would seem that we owe it to ourselves to question the validity of at least some of its assumptions. And ultimately we must ask ourselves: Is there a concept of economics that is consistent with an ecological worldview? If so, what is it?"

The answers to Gary's questions regarding a form of economics consistent with an ecological worldview are still only slowly emerging. But back in the 1980s, the New Alchemists were gamely ready to tackle them. In some ways, the early '80s proved the busiest in years. The number of annual visitors averaged ten thousand. The masthead of the annual report for 1982 listed a staff of twenty-one with eleven apprentices. In spite of the inevitable skirmishes, constructive ideas and new incentives were emerging from the collective soul-searching. These were efforts that, in Christina Rawley's words, "were aimed at decreasing our financial vulnerability and our dependence on federal grants and contracts." Reluctantly we raised the price of membership. We also stepped up our publishing efforts. At Gary's initiative we signed a publishing contract for a series of "how to" books. As we were seeing more than seven thousand visitors over the summer, and Rob Sardinsky had been touring up to three thousand students during the school year, we also thought we could expand on-site education to generate more income and began to draw up new programs in that area as well.

The changing economic climate next led us to reevaluate our major financial Achilles heel: the money being drained off in rent payments for the land every month—with no prospect of our ever seeing any return. The only remedy seemed to be to tighten our collective belt and buy all 12 acres. Our investigations indicated that mortgage payments would consume 10 percent of our operating costs, which represented a huge commitment. Knowing full well that it would be a heavy and ongoing burden, we nonetheless decided to buy the Farm from our landlords, Bob and Anita Gunning. This not only affected our fund-raising, it also served to make us more sensitive to our connection to the land and to the larger community and to ground us on Cape Cod. At Gary's and Greg Watson's instigation, New Alchemy became a founding member of the Cape and Islands Self-Reliance Coalition, a still existing cooperative organization dedicated not only to energy conservation but to bringing the appropriate tools and information about self-reliance and sustainability to the low-income households most in need of it.

In spite of everyone's redoubled efforts at generating support, fund-raising remained an unrelenting challenge. Over the years all of us involved tended to identify with Sisyphus of Greek mythology: doomed to roll a great stone uphill for all eternity. Gary reached that point after two years at the helm. He had been feeling for some time that total immersion in proposal writing and fund-raising was not the way he chose to serve our common cause. As soon as he could be replaced, he moved on to the world of enterprise to lead his Stonyfield Farms to the prominent position it occupies today.

After a brief and very unhappy intermediate interlude with a director we had recruited from outside the group, Research Director John Quinney stepped into the breach. The only person both the staff and the board thought equal to the job, he became the fourth, and after John Todd, the longest-serving director of New Alchemy. It was no small task he had taken on. In spite of cutbacks, just meeting payroll was an ongoing challenge. But John Quinney shared Gary's conviction that the time had come for the Institute to prove itself economically, and he led a re-markably successful campaign to raise money from the private sector. Gradually things began to improve. A challenge grant from one foundation, for example, was met with such a prompt response from Institute members and supporters that it was answered six months ahead of schedule. In addition, we began to see a marked increase in earned income. Fees from the education programs and mem-bership, publication and produce sales, and consulting work reached 30 percent of total income. This latter figure spoke volumes about the level of effort being put forth not only by John Quinney but by the entire staff.

Major Restructuring

To further adapt to the times, John Quinney and the New Alchemy staff consulted with the Technical Development Corporation (TDC) to help in what John called the "exciting and at times painful process of goals definition and reorganization." As could be expected, TDC recommended total restructuring of what editor Kate Eldred, who had taken over publications, called "our old, friendly, non-hierarchical setup." In the new *New Alchemy Quarterly*, which had replaced the *Journal*, Kate explained, "We were to construct a real board of directors with power to hire the executive director; to form a management group with real powers; to make man-agers responsible for those in their section; and to set up realistic budgets."

The details were hashed out in marathon meetings. New Alchemy would focus on two priorities: enhancing household food, energy, water, and waste systems; and researching small farm systems based on year-round vegetable and small fruit production. The regional focus was to be the northeastern United States. New Alchemy and TDC together produced a draft mission statement: "The New Alchemy Institute is an environmental science center that provides tools and information to sustain household and small farm economies. The Institute's services include research, demonstration and education projects in food, energy, water, and waste treatment." It was a far cry from our original "To restore the lands, protect the seas, and inform the Earth's stewards."

Kate summarized the process: "Forging a hierarchy out of a consensus model was a painful and exhilarating task. On the negative side, tempers flared, accusations of demagoguery and dictatorship abounded, and old alliances were severed. On the positive side, people who were committed to projects found that their budgets were honored, that evaluations took place on time, and that the outside world could count on reaching the people who were doing the job." New Alchemy's collaboration with TDC was the most dramatic indication of the shifts that were taking place. Partly the result of Reaganomics, it was essentially a survival tactic. Still, it was viewed as a controversial and precipitous move. Some people saw it as a sign that the Institute was losing its way. That our goals and restructuring were being defined by outsiders was an indication of the degree of revisionism that had taken place. It was an abnegation of self-definition that would have been an anathema to the early New Alchemy. We may have been woefully in need of streamlining then, but we had no doubts about who we were and what we were to try to do in the world. Still, as Bill McLarney commented, "As long as ethical concern for the fate of the planet remains an everyday reality, it will still be New Alchemy."

Pushing On with the Research

In spite of all the recalibrating, as long as the National Science Foundation funding lasted, the aquaculture team pressed on toward greater levels of integration of the energy and biological systems. The grant had been awarded to fund the research of the aquaculture team, made up of John Todd, Ron Zweig, Al Doolittle, John Wolfe, and Dave Engstrom. As stated earlier, the goal of the research was to evaluate the potential of the solar-algae ponds and to develop ecological models of their internal dynamics. It was to be a further step in gaining an understanding of whole systems with the ultimate goal of determining the conditions that would lead to maximum productivity. In this consolidation of earlier work, New Alchemy was treading a fine line between well-tested and innovative strategies. Among the most innovative then was the incorporation of computers as biological monitors. Computers, in fact, were becoming a central means of communicating with our living systems. Equally essential were their interpreters Al, Joe, and John Wolfe. Debate of whether we ought to be using computers was ancient history; once we had monitors installed and operational in both Arks, we felt it was time to come out of the closet.

"It may come as a shock, or at the least as a surprise, to some of our readers," Al reported, "to learn that New Alchemy has acquired two computers. We use our microcomputers to design data acquisition and control programs that collect and store data for later analysis. We also have programs to analyze and plot the data. We are not trying to replace ourselves as observers and participants in our experiments, but we do use them to read instruments and turn on pumps, open valves, and control vents. They cannot smell, taste, or see, but they can measure temperature, pH, sunlight, humidity, dissolved oxygen, and many other physical parameters twenty-four hours a day. We are not designing environments that require a computer for maintenance, but we do see it as a useful tool for studying complex systems."

John Wolfe had earlier made his *Journal* debut with an article entitled "On the Cryptic Phrase Mathematical Modeling." "A mathematical model is a set of mathematical statements that describe the relationships between elements in a system," he wrote. He went on to list the purposes that could be served by robust mathematical models:

1. Organize and tie together knowledge.
2. Reveal the logical implications of that knowledge.
3. Direct research by pointing out which important relationships are not yet well defined.
4. Guide action by showing how changes in particular relationships or elements affect the rest of the system.

Explaining that the team had chosen systems dynamics as the most appropriate mathematical tool for analyzing the ecosystems in bioshelters, John Wolfe reported that Colleen Armstrong, for one, had started collecting data on aphid outbreaks in the Cape Cod Ark. In our first attempt to model integrated pest management, she was tracking the effectiveness of a fungal parasite in controlling aphids. The computers were also in on a race among New Alchemists to create the most productive solar ponds and were churning out mathematical solutions.

One of the most loved and respected leaders of the environmental movement, Donella Meadows, who had trained John Wolfe at Dartmouth College, was solidly behind the NSF team's approach to their electronic colleague. In the seventh *Journal* she wrote, "I've been involved with or an advisor to projects using computer simulation in many fields for many purposes. I often lecture to my students about the ideal process of give and take between the model builder and the model user. But I have never seen that ideal achieved—except at New Alchemy. There John Wolfe has managed to keep his models transparent, directed to the actual problems, and flexible to the changing knowledge and concerns of the group. This has transmitted a growing understanding of feedback structure and system dynamics to the others at NAI, while they were transmitting to them their knowledge, ideas, and hunches about aquaculture systems. The staff has been open to this new method of integrating their insights, constructively critical as the model evolved and alert to discrepancies between model predictions and real events. The result is a model that is an effective communication tool, with which chemists, zoologists, and engineers can point out the connections among light penetration, ammonia concentration, and fish growth. New experiments can be designed and tested both in the model and in the solar ponds. And there is a tighter link between theory and practice than I have ever seen elsewhere, a fast cycling between the deductive and inductive phases of the scientific method. It really warms the heart of a modeling proponent like me to see just once this powerful tool used with the right mixture of skepticism and enthusiasm, and with frequent checks back and forth between the model and the real world."

The modeling became particularly pertinent to the NSF team when, after several years of operation, they were finding that even the solar ponds were subject to limits to growth: "After several years of monitoring fish growth in solar-algae ponds, it began to seem as though we were coming up against a ceiling. We could grow fish rapidly for a short time or slowly for long periods of time. But we could not achieve optimal growth. The difficulty lay in maintaining balanced water chemistry. Most serious was the buildup of toxic ammonia. Experimenting with a series of variables, they devised a range of methods for maintaining water quality: improving algal assimilation of ammonia, phosphate, and carbon dioxide by increasing the settling rate of suspended particulates; adding a nitrifying bacterial filter to the system; increasing the exchange of nutrient-laden water with freshwater; and transferring organic material to a settling tank. They found this auxiliary tank extended the period of good water chemistry from six to twenty weeks. They continued to hone their systems for the duration of the NSF funding. The understanding of aquatic ecosystems gleaned from them is still fundamental to the unfolding of ecological design.

Toward the end of its first decade, New Alchemy underwent an examination that gave us an objective assessment of where we stood when the Rockefeller Brothers Fund, one of our major supporters, commissioned a report to evaluate our "operational effectiveness, progress and impact." The investigation was conducted by the husband and wife team of Barbara and David Hertz, working in conjunction with Dr. Barry Valentine of Ohio State University as science adviser. The Hertzes had approached New Alchemy, in their own words, "with a great deal of skepticism." They came away, their report continued, "with a cautiously optimistic view of the potential contribution of NAI, and a genuine feeling of good, though unorthodox, scientific work being done." They found our "esprit to be of the highest order." Dr. Valentine had also felt dubious until he encountered the working reality. As a scientist he understood the paradoxical nature of our scientific position. "The Ark is a man-made [sic] ecosystem and they are just beginning to learn how to maintain it. The experimental procedures may involve intuition, data are often observational not meristic, predictability is often low, and uncontrolled variability may be high. There is a body of scientists who downgrade this kind of research. These individuals do not understand that the reduction of experimental variables (for example, isolation in a climate-controlled chamber to stabilize temperature and humidity) introduces many new biotic variables resulting from the absence of interacting organisms. I'm saying that the holistic approach of the Institute is realistic, practical, and approximates nature, but it is very disturbing to the scientist who thinks that if you break up a very complex and interrelated problem into its smaller isolated components, solve each, and then reconstitute the many solutions into one, the result will solve the original problem. Biotic systems just do not work that way. I think that the Institute has a real scientific base and is investigating an incredibly difficult project."

The research staff of that period was on a strong learning curve in other areas as well. Thanks to John Quinney's persistent efforts, after a hiatus of a few years, we once again received an influx of government funding. As a result of a new initiative, referred to as LISA (low-input sustainable agriculture), New Alchemy received a U.S. Department of Agriculture grant to participate in a small farm research, demonstration, and outreach program. The demonstration included cover crop trials, integrated pest management, a composting greenhouse, and information distribution.

In addition to a newly established Research Associates program, New Alchemy was taking on an outreach effort that harked back to the Readers Research program of the early years. The Institute was asking Cape Cod gardeners to participate in a project aimed at reduction of pesticide use and expansion of the database for sustainable agriculture. Through what they were calling the Habitat Program, New Alchemists were turning to organic gardeners in the area to gather data and learn more about beneficial insects. With an ironic appropriateness of which he was acutely aware, the Research Associate taking charge of the program went by the name of Robert Bugg. Under his direction, local gardeners were to observe and keep records in the manner of classical natural historians. Their specific assignment was to plant insect habitats, monitor insect populations, and report on their findings. Participants were given a list of annuals and biennials to choose from. They were to monitor the comings and goings of parasitic wasps, flies, green lacewings, assassin bugs, and minute pirate bugs. The data gathered added to New Alchemy's as well as the participants' understanding of the Cape as a bioregion.

In the bioshelters and in the gardens we were pressing on with further biological pest control. Colleen Armstrong was investigating entomogenous (insect-eating) nematodes for cabbage maggot and other pests. She was also still monitoring the effectiveness of using *Aphidoletes aphidimyza* in doing battle with aphids. As her IPM research gained recognition, Colleen became involved in a pilot project for a local commercial greenhouse. The objective was to establish and demonstrate an IPM program for potted chrysanthemums and to introduce growers to pest management methods in order to reduce pesticide applications. Her primary target pest was four species of thrips. A predacious mite, *Amblyseius cucumeris*, proved effective in curtailing one of the thrips species in the commercial arena.

Biological controls were also of interest to a number of other New Alchemists, who were planning to take these proactive measures to the larger community and involve farmers in nematode research. Staff entomologist Dave Simser obtained a grant from the Massachusetts Cranberry Growers Association to see how realistic it was to apply biological controls to cranberries. He reported in the *Quarterly*: "It gave us the chance to work with a new grower group, new pests, and new crops and to use classical biological techniques within a bog against a major pest known as the cranberry fruitworm." His strategy was to release thousands of parasitic wasps, *Trichogramma pretiosum*, to coincide with the egg stage of the fruitworm. He thought that if the cranberry industry could develop ways to reduce its use of pesticides and herbicides without sacrificing yields, bogs could continue to be significant providers of employment and revenue, and cranberry acres would remain a valuable component of open space conservation. The current availability of organic cranberries in the market attests to the viability of such research.

A Milestone Ahead of Its Time

Sadly, the same steady consolidation of efforts that we applied to pest control could not be claimed for the research on Prince Edward Island. After its triumphant debut, the Island Ark was beset with problems. They had nothing to do with the performance of the structure, which, like its Cape counterpart, was more than proving itself. The redundancy of the whole system approach to climate control was quickly justified. Overall homeostasis of the internal climate was maintained through the symbiosis of architectural, biological, and electronic design. This was indisputable after the building weathered a three-day storm with below-zero temperatures and winds in excess of 40 miles an hour. With the Island utility down for the duration, it was the stored solar warmth in the solar-algae ponds that saved the day. Joe Seale estimated they must have released an estimated 1 million BTUs (British Thermal Units) to maintain a safe internal climate in the food-growing areas.

Not only were the solar-algae ponds offering an unexpected bonus by acting as reliable, low-temperature furnaces, as on the Cape, they were proving remarkably productive in fulfilling their primary purpose of growing fish—in this case, excellent crops of healthy and locally popular trout. In the horticultural area, Nancy Willis was using diversified soil building and maintenance methods similar to those in the Cape Ark. Even as North Atlantic winds blew over the icy waters of the Northumberland Strait, she was growing healthy crops of lettuce, kale, spinach, chard, broccoli, parsley, beans, herbs, and flowers at a commercial level.

With the aid of his microcomputers, Al Doolittle had devised a monitoring regimen to match precisely the needs of the Ark's subsystems. As a result, we had immediate feedback on the dynamics of the building's metabolism. His work was intended to interface the human, biological, and electronic controls so that a relatively inexperienced bioshelter resident could be trained by the systems without having to worry that his or her inexperience might lead to failure in any major subcomponent. We were also using the Ark to consider designs and applications for other geographic regions. With the Hydrowind we were also on a learning curve. Research in wind-generated electrical production was moving rapidly, and better, simpler machines were becoming available. Joe Seale reported on our trials with the Hydrowind, explaining that although it was living up to its original criteria in delivering the wind component of the Ark's natural energy systems, it would require "substantial design simplifications to meet criteria for low cost maintenance."

But, as ever, money—or the lack of it—cast a shadow. The Canadian government had made a commitment to build the Ark but not to maintain it. After the initial grants, we were both underfunded and understaffed to fulfill our goals in research, education, and public service. John made several trips to Ottawa to try to garner more support, but it proved impossible to raise enough money for us to keep the Ark going on our own. As we were wrestling with our financial shortfall, we learned that Andrew Wells, who had first introduced John's ideas into government circles, had founded a new organization—the Institute for Man [sic] and Resources—which was to be based on his native Prince Edward Island. (I hadn't gotten to Wells with my pitch about sexist language in time, and among ourselves we referred to his organization as the Institute for Bleep and Resources.) Its philosophy and program was remarkably similar to ours. Unfortunately, as an indigenous organization, it was also a formidable competitor for Canadian government funding. Our support was reduced, as John put it, "enough to cripple us but not to kill us."

After long hours of pondering, we hit on a compromise solution. Andy Wells's group was in a much better position geographically and financially to carry on the work on the Island. Reluctantly, we decided we had to turn management and fund-raising for the Ark over to the Institute for Man and Resources. We remained responsible for the scientific research, and Nancy Willis stayed on to coordinate the agriculture program. It was a compromise that partially rescued the research but fell far short of our early hopes, and John and Nancy were devastated.

In 1981, we received the ultimate blow. Throughout the management tenure of the Institute of Man and Resources, we had maintained a mutually useful flow of research information between the staffs of the two Arks. But after elections that year our Canadian allies were out of office in both federal and provincial governments. At that point all financial support was withdrawn. The building so wholeheartedly dedicated to "Weaving together the sun, wind, biology, and architecture on behalf of humanity" was not considered politically expedient, and the doors of the Canadian Ark were closed. It was not until 2000 that it was rediscovered, at least conceptually. That year, along with such landmarks as the Empire State Building and McDonald's golden arches, the U.S. Department of Energy recognized "'John Todd's Ark' as one of the milestone buildings of the twentieth century."

The Semester and New Education Programs

Fortunately, we were not so vulnerable on the Cape, at least not politically, as we were on the Island. In 1984, New Alchemy launched its most ambitious education program to date. Over the years our apprenticeship program had taken many forms, with the numbers of participants ranging from four to forty, and there were always more requests than we could accommodate. That year we decided to supplement it with a semester-length combination of formal classes and fieldwork, which would offer an optimal focus for New Alchemy's specialized resources.

Education director Greg Watson had moved off to a position in state government, and Merryl Alber, a very bright young biologist, was in charge of the logistics. Collaborating with Lesley College in Boston and the National Audubon's Expedition Institute, she put together a program in biological agriculture and appropriate technology. Students completing the course could receive up to sixteen credits through Lesley College and Audubon or make comparable arrangements with their own colleges or universities. The Semester Program was geared toward students in their junior year. It lasted for sixteen weeks, from the end of January through mid-May. New Alchemy staff and adjunct faculty taught the courses. The number of students varied from year to year, with the average being about twelve. The curriculum fell into four basic areas of study: biological agriculture and appropriate technology; ecosystem design; bioregional planning; and applied studies in ecological design.

By the Semester's second year Merryl herself had gone back in school to study for her PhD, so Earle Barnhart took over as education director. He decided to expose the students to as much of New Alchemy's information and general approach as possible. The first day of classes, they assembled and sealed microcosms of plants, animals, and soil life. As the weeks went on, students grew commercial-scale garden lettuce, greenhouse tomatoes, hydroponic lettuce on top of solar ponds, and edible mushrooms in our experimental composting greenhouse. In midspring, instructor and students went foraging for a bioregional meal of local spring foods that included a wide range of wild edibles. These experiences were evidence that one of the goals of the semester was being met—hands-on experience with living systems and an understanding of the pulses and flows of energy and nutrients in ecosystems.

Based on their feedback, the Semester was offering something the students genuinely valued. One of them, Deb Grubin, reported to her adviser at Beloit College: "In all of the classes, the first thing to be discussed was whole systems and how what we would be studying fit into a systems perspective, how everything we were learning was connected. In my case I had been feeling tormented by my lack of vision, basically due to lack of experience or having spent the past few years not trusting anything not based on the Newtonian/Cartesian paradigm, no matter how much I disagreed with it. At New Alchemy I took the plunge and immersed myself in an environment where systemic and non-linear or intuitive thinking were respected and supported. At first I had to learn to trust myself. I was learning that something understood first intuitively should be possible to explain logically and rationally. A semi-closed ecosystem designed to recycle as much as possible for the purpose of growing food sounded right to my sense of aesthetics. Is it as sound realistically? At New Alchemy ideas like this are put to rigorous testing and monitoring."

Although Semester students, Research Associates, volunteers, and troops of children were then surging purposefully around the Farm, the apprentices or interns were still an important sector of both the work and the social dynamic of the place. Peter Williams, who rose from intern to head gardener in a single year, recorded his impressions in the *New Alchemy Quarterly*: "Apprentice," he mused, "isn't that one notch above indentured servant? Why did I get up at six thirty every morning to work for free? Why did I quit a paying job to make room for volunteering? And what is an apprentice anyhow? Just another field hand? No. I think not. To apprentice is to first acknowledge that there is something bigger than yourself. It acknowledges one's position in a process and a tradition. It's a humbling and an empowering experience. You apprentice yourself to something, not someone. I wasn't the gardener's apprentice. I was the garden's apprentice."

The educational goals of the New Alchemists did not stop with the experiences of the interns or Semester Program. Beginning with a popular series of summer workshops for children, comparative newcomers Kim Knorr and Debbie Habib decided to continue them on Saturdays throughout the year. Young, gentle, and soft-spoken, both women were at heart closet educational reformers. In affiliation with Falmouth school officials they set up a program geared to be complementary to the fourth grade science curriculum. As with their summer workshops, Kim and Debbie focused the program to further the fourth graders' understanding of natural systems. They wrote of their educational philosophy: "We approach education with the belief that we need to teach children a sense of individual responsibility, environmental awareness, and practical living skills. We discuss how the weather is changing, where the leaves are going, and what the animals are doing. We study various soil types. We discuss the geological history and soil structure of the Cape and how that relates to water pollution and growing food. Science is no longer something confined to men in white coats in a lab. We are taking children and teachers out of the classroom into a natural setting, exposing them to new ways to think about the natural environment, and teaching them some basics in primary processes. For many of us children spark the hope for a better future. Their simplicity, curiosity, wonder and desire to explore the world reminds us of the qualities we often lose touch with in our daily lives."

Earle recounted New Alchemy pedagogy as follows: "It's tough promoting long-term thinking and understanding of whole systems when the economic system of our time strives to maximize short-term profit. And it's a struggle to help preserve the biological integrity of the Earth in a political climate that converts much of our society into weapons systems. But we feel that major cultural changes must be promoted and that everyone is ultimately involved. The cumulative power of small personal choices produces global effects and we believe that better personal choices can reverse some of the current destructive world trends. So in our education programs, we nurture the ability to express one's detailed vision of the future—in landscape designs, in career decisions, and in daily personal choices.

Preserving the health of the Earth and educating human minds appear to be mutually necessary tasks."

In addition to the on-site programs, almost all the New Alchemists at some point also taught courses or gave workshops at various schools, colleges, conferences, and alternative institutions, planting seeds of New Alchemy ideas, both literally and figuratively. With all of these efforts and the Semester Program well established, throughout the 1980s New Alchemy's educational program achieved a new level of excellence. Although we had been reaching out to people for many years, the results had been well intentioned but piecemeal. In our early years we as aptly could have called ourselves a research and learning rather than a research and education organization. Still, if the fierce idealism and leading-edge scientific inquiry of that time had shifted toward economic credibility and pragmatism, the New Alchemists of the 1980s put the experience of fifteen years to work to achieve a unique and cohesive program that was the culmination of the Institute's educational work. Reviewing its track record, John Quinney mused, "Perhaps providing an environment for training, sharing experiences, and enhancing knowledge for an ecological future is our major achievement. Perhaps our most successful crop is people."

chapter nine

Victims of Our
Own Success

Let ours be a time remembered for the awakening of a new
reverence for life, the firm resolve to achieve sustainability,
the quickening of the struggle for justice and peace,
and the joyful celebration of life.
—The Earth Charter

Although most of us who spent time at New Alchemy truly believed in trying to integrate our values into our individual lives, one conspicuous discrepancy in how we were going about it had been bothering some of us. For years we had found ourselves distinctly ill at ease when visitors to the Farm would enthuse about what they were seeing. Impressed with the various bioshelters, they were inclined to say things such as, "All this is so wonderful. I suppose you live like this at home too?" It was awkward for us, because, in the main, we did not and we were uncomfortable about it. There we were advocating alternatives in energy and shelter, but we were not yet practicing what we preached.

Then, over the winter of 1979, Denise Backus, whose perceptive warmth helped us all through bumpy periods and whose desk in the front office had become the nerve center of the place, began to sense a shift in the wind. Piecing together scraps from various conversations, she came up with the news that a number of New Alchemy households were about to go solar. Of course many of us had talked on and off about doing so for years, but by the end of 1980 we had done so. Hilde Maingay and Earle Barnhart added a bioshelter to their pre–World War II house near Woods Hole. They did the design and most of the construction themselves. Hilde wrote of their new solar space: "It is

The Todd house with solar retrofit.

winter vacation. Flowering geraniums, impatiens, and nasturtiums. A summer bouquet in winter. Sitting at the table, I can stretch my arm to pick a big salad for dinner. The kids play a game of cards in tee shirts. Laughter and red warm faces."

Ardent gardeners, Denise and her oceanographer husband, Richard Backus, had a house of about the same vintage as Hilde and Earle's and also opted for an attached greenhouse. They had already taken energy efficiency about as far as they could with insulation, nightshades, and curtains. Although they were doing well in conserving heat, with living room and kitchen windows all facing south, they knew they could do better. With a lot of scrounging and recycling and do-it-yourself construction, they built their greenhouse for about $250. Denise reported, "It warms the house, gives us alpine strawberries all winter long, and it pleases the eye. It brings us into direct contact with our physical surroundings and makes us feel more alive."

John Todd and I also succumbed to the solar trend but, after weighing our options, did not confine ourselves to a greenhouse. Our house had begun life as a late 1960s ticky-tacky Cape Codder. Although pretty with its steep rooflines and shingles, it had no insulation. It was not the sort of house that lent credibility to our advocacy of sustainable living. We went to our friend, architect Malcolm Wells, with the stipulation that we wanted our fantasized addition to "fit" in terms of lines and feel with the rest of the house. Joe Seale and John Wolfe designed the energy system. After six months of living amid construction—Rebecca

The Todd greenhouse from the living room.

was wont to bemoan, "I want to go home but they've taken it away!"—we had our house transformed just in time for a family gathering to celebrate John's father's seventieth birthday. Today, it is no longer state-of-the-art in terms of energy efficiency, but we have loved every day in it, and the greenhouse has been the incubator in which John's innumerable inventions get their first trials.

Ron Zweig and Christina Rawley were the only "Alchies" to build a solar house from scratch or, as they phrased it, "from the ground up." The result was charming. Although not large, the ingenious use of space and high ceilings for air convection gave it an airy and roomy feel. It was designed so that the greenhouse was the major source of heat. The solar-algae ponds there gave Ron a place to grow enormous hydroponic lettuces as well as fish. Summer dinners on their deck overlooking the pond, accompanied by the deep-throated serenade of bullfrogs, were one of our favorite seasonal rituals. Ron and Christina, like the rest of us, were happy not only with their solar improvement on the home front but even more to be living more closely in line with our rhetoric.

Our solar houses had long been in order by 1985 when New Alchemy took time off to celebrate its fifteenth anniversary. As the gala day approached, the accustomed buzz of normal summer activity escalated to full roar. Somehow word had spread like wildfire. Even people we thought we had lost track of over the years had gotten the message. By the eve of August 18 almost six hundred of us had gathered at the Farm, with more, as it turned out, still on the way.

We were rewarded with a beautiful, ripe, summer day. A solar café in the Ark did a land office trade, with ongoing music and food that ranged from homegrown organic to Mexican to Native American. The workshops were equally varied, ranging over the usual New Alchemy fare to socially responsible investment, earth shelter, and grassroots political action. Area businesses had a strong presence, as did Cape-based organizations involved in social and environmental issues. There was a daylong kids' program with a show featuring a ventriloquist, not to mention a big birthday cake. Ernest Callenbach, the author of *Ecotopia*, gave the keynote address, bravely maintaining—in the heyday of Reagonomics—that the state of ecosystems and not economics should be the major criterion for judging the actions of a society.

The highlight of the day was an informal plenary session during which the reunited Alchies were invited to give an update on their activities to the larger group. Everyone had interesting developments to report. We had fanned out into a number of walks of life. We had become farmers and landscapers, energy analysts, business people, and cyberneticists. One former Alchemist declared himself a born-again redneck. But it was Christina who stole the show. She had never been happy with the level of New Alchemy's capitulation to the economic imperative of Reaganism. She felt that too many of the ideals of the founding generation had been swept aside and some of our greatest strengths, such as the aquaculture and wind programs, prematurely buried. The early New Alchemy had always had a deep internalized sense of purpose, yet one of the workshops that day had been devoted to inviting suggestions from the public for future directions for the Institute. Christina bridled at this lack of self-definition. This, combined with an excessive feeling of self-congratulation she felt in the air, could only be countered with farce. Her distress mounted with the tenor of the day. In the midst of the testimonials, she found herself summoning all her skills as an actor to register her protest.

As the rest of us were sitting or standing on the grass in a semicircle facing the crowd, Christina lurched back into the group. Usually immaculate, she was almost unrecognizable as she staggered toward us in tattered bathrobe and slippers, bedecked in curlers and smeared makeup. Clutching a glass of Scotch in one hand and a cigarette in the other, she shrilled, "Is the revolution over yet?" I shifted over to make room for her as she approached, and she settled beside me, ranting and cackling. Brandishing the ceremonial drink of her Scottish forebears, she carried on for a bit longer, then quieted. But she had made her point. Those striving for acceptance and respectability in the perceived reality of the 1980s were horrified. Here was the wild, the unplanned, the joker, once again in our midst. The rest of us recognized the timely arrival of a shaman. The need for the unsummoned, uncontrollable, but still feisty feminine element, which would never capitulate to loss of connection with life's underlying essentials, was as urgent as anything else that was said or done that day.

Another reflection of how we felt came from Conn Nugent, who after his time with us went on to become the executive director of the Noble Peace Prize–winning Physicians against Nuclear War (now Physicians for Social Responsibility). He also spoke to everyone's experience: "The nicest part about coming back is feeling good about it. The people we met here endure as friends. The ideals that propelled us here continue to propel us after being here and endure. I don't know anyone who has worked at New Alchemy for any significant period of time who is not proud of having been here. And me too."

"And me too," most of us echoed silently, swallowing the lumps in our throats.

A Passing and a Fading of the Torch

At the time of our anniversary celebration, and even as the 1980s were drawing to a close, it still felt as though New Alchemy was finding new strengths on which to build. The financial burden of being director of a nonprofit, however, was beginning to wear on John Quinney, and he was feeling a need to move on. He had kept the Institute operating in the black since 1984. But like Gary Hirshberg before him, John was ready to test some of his ideas in the rough-and-tumble of the marketplace. John's departure was an unsettling, if not entirely unanticipated, development for staff and board alike. Artist and activist Judy Barnett, who was then president of the board of directors, responded, "I was worried that this might happen on my watch." John had warned us about funding prospects: "Unless the Institute can make a significant profit on retail sales, memberships, education programs, or some other activities it will remain in a financially precarious position."

By the summer of 1989 the search for a new director was on. The board, led by Judy Barnet and a selection committee, met frequently. The new executive director had to be someone familiar with the Institute, not only intellectually but also with our still somewhat unorthodox organizational ways of doing things. Our dilemma resolved itself with unexpected ease when Greg Watson applied for the job. He was still very much part of the fabric of the Institute, and during his six-year stint in state government had remained a close and influential friend. Extraordinarily bright and visionary, and as familiar with New Alchemy ways as with the air he breathed, Greg was a perfect fit for the next executive director.

That autumn the torch was formally passed from John Quinney to Greg. The conceptual continuity of the transition in leadership was reflected in their statements at the time. John summarized New Alchemy's past: "We began with the ecological ideas of the founders and schemes tested in backyard ponds and funky greenhouses. Over the years we gained staff and attracted more and more visitors, received recognition from many sources, survived the departure of our founders, the inevitable differences of opinion, the times of no funding, and the warped priorities of the Reagan administration. Through it all we remained ever mindful of the need for research and education in ecological practices as we designed and built structures, landscapes, fishponds, and farms. We have changed, often testing the fuzzy line between ecological idealism and economic pragmatism. We have learned not to confuse progress toward an ecological future with that future itself."

Greg took up the narrative with a statement that holds as true in the first decades of the twenty-first century as it did in 1989: "We know how to grow food without poisoning the land or water supplies. We understand that it is possible to provide society's energy needs without recourse to fossil fuels or nuclear energy. We have learned how to design manufacturing processes that do not pose a threat to the health of factory workers or to the environment. We also know that our best chance at averting a devastatingly abrupt change in global climate depends on adopting these strategies as soon as possible. The number one priority for many poor people in this country and in developing nations around the world is to raise their standard of living. The next major challenge, given the uncertainty that still surrounds the social and cultural aspects of this concept, will be to discover how to mobilize society to work towards sustainability. We have to tackle these socio-economic issues with the same determination that, for the past twenty years, has been focused on developing alternatives to technologies that pollute or otherwise degrade the environment."

Greg Watson's tenure as New Alchemy's director began in 1990 with little sense of the shadow that was soon to fall. We felt that another transition had been weathered, and we once again had a charismatic and articulate leader. A more critical assessment could perhaps have given some premonition of what was to come. A number of the grants that had helped carry the Institute over the past several years had run their course. Still, it was generally felt that we had been through so much that somehow we would find our way. Why not? It was a time when it seemed that almost anything could happen. Over recent months we had seen the end of the Soviet Empire, the crumbling of the Berlin Wall, and the end of single-party rule in Russia. There had been candlelit faces singing in Wenceslas Square in Prague to celebrate Czechoslovakia's velvet revolution. With the release of Nelson Mandela after years of imprisonment, the rebirth of hope leapfrogged from Europe to South Africa and around the world. Surely New Alchemy would muddle through the 1990s.

Our optimism proved short-lived. As the handwriting on the wall became clearer, hints appeared in the *Quarterly,* revealing a "cash crunch." New Alchemy admitted to being in fiscal crisis, citing "a temporary but severe income shortage." Greg was quoted as saying, "A sluggish regional economy, combined with increased competition for foundation support has caused a serious shortfall in revenues this year." We had become, as he wryly phrased it, "victims of our own success." He went on to explain, "We have fallen upon hard times just as the established scientific community is acknowledging the validity of our work and vision. This may seem ironic but it is not totally unpredictable."

As could be expected, as uncertainty mounted and the money shortage was more acutely felt, there were internal problems as well. Greg's all-encompassing vision and goals did not always sit well with some of the staff—or the board. He saw a need to look beyond the more narrowly focused, economically oriented policies that had evolved in the years he had been gone. He understood that the ideas that had been seen as innovative only a few years before were being more broadly accepted scientifically and academically. New Alchemy was in a position analogous to that of land grant colleges and some university departments. And competition for funding was much fiercer. He felt strongly that to win back foundation interest New Alchemy had to return to the cutting edge in both vision and mission.

Few on either the staff or the board agreed with Greg. Because John and I were moving in the same circles in fund-raising for Ocean Arks, we understood his position—and his frustrations. Like us, he had spent time conferring with foundation people and knew there were changes in the wind. Greg saw urban areas and the inner cities as ripe for New Alchemy ideas, but the staff strongly resisted this direction. It was not part of the program painstakingly delineated with the consulting group not so long ago. Some of the staff argued that we did not have any answers that applied to city problems. Greg did not maintain that we had answers as such. He did think that we had a background that gave us the equivalent of a compass with which we could calibrate our knowledge to almost any situation. Both staff and board were finding themselves at a growing impasse. It was rumored both inside and beyond the group that New Alchemy had lost much of its spirit and élan.

It was a very unhappy period. The desire to understand one another's differing points of view never wavered, but the center of the stalemate lay in the fact that Greg and a few others saw little future in the current direction of the Institute. The rest had no faith or little interest in the course he saw as viable. Board meetings were tense and frustrating. My private journal notes after one meeting read, "Painful! Hard as hell. But lots of good will and guts and kindness on the part of most people. It's too soon to give up."

For Greg, deliverance came unexpectedly when he was nominated Massachusetts Commissioner of Food and Agriculture. It was an excellent position for him, as his position at New Alchemy had become close to untenable. Because opinion was divided, and also because we were so uncertain as to what lay ahead, the board agreed that Greg take a leave of absence.

Closure

With Greg's departure, the board asked New Alchemy's education director, Virginia Rasmussen, to serve as acting executive director, and she bravely took on the job at a moment that was hardly auspicious. For all the intelligence, good will, and determination that Virginia and the remaining staff were bringing to bear, the prospects for the Institute remained bleak. They stepped up the pace on getting out proposals and drawing up a prospectus on projected programs. Money in the form of donations, small grants, and a fair response to the annual appeal continued to arrive. But it was daily becoming evident that prospective income from small research grants and the various programs fell far below the level necessary for the mortgage and the most basic maintenance of the land and the building, let alone staff salaries.

By early 1991 Virginia had to report that the results of the latest round of fundraising efforts had been disappointing. Feelers put out by other board members to determine outside perception of the Institute were bringing equally unwelcome news. We were told that the times were passing us by, that New Alchemy's work was no longer seen as indispensable. Slowly, among board members at least, financial reality began to undermine increasingly unfounded hope.

One night in January 1991 I received a call from Judy announcing that she was afraid that the end was in sight. My response was to agree. It had become clear to me that the New Alchemy story had been told. It was, in retrospect, a turning point for me. From then on I was in favor of moving as quickly as possible to bring about as graceful a closure as we could muster. I described the next board meeting in my journal as "dreary and sad." I am not sure why or how I, or any of us on the board, managed to stick it out. But I think we agreed that not to have done so would have been irresponsible, perhaps dishonorable.

Discussions began to shift from whether we should close to how it might be done. Was there a realistic option that could rescue the Institute financially? Once again deliverance was at hand, and after the details were ironed out, the perfect resolution presented itself. For several years Hilde Maingay and Earle Barnhart had been involved in discussions about starting an environmental cohousing community that would try to recapture the communal support systems, common spaces, and shared facilities of traditional villages. Both of them had been pivotal to New Alchemy for many years. Like most of us, they had never lost their love and loyalty for the place. By that time they had a successful ecological landscaping business called the Great Work, and were ready for their next step. Of course they were privy to unfolding events at New Alchemy. That they might take over the site seemed almost too good to be true. They had the vision and contacts with people interested in starting a community. We had the land and some of the buildings for them to get started. Another round of discussions began. Bankers and lawyers were consulted. Cautious optimism hovered.

We weathered the inevitable negotiations. In May 1991 the board had in hand a draft of a purchase and sale agreement between the New Alchemy Institute and Cape Cohousing. Judy prepared the press releases in June: "The board of directors of the New Alchemy Institute has announced that the Institute will close its doors as soon as its affairs can be concluded. Financial conditions led to the sale of the organization's facilities, making it possible to pay all obligations and finish in the black." The *Cape Cod Times* responded graciously: "Like many another praise-worthy non-profit private enterprise, the New Alchemy Institute has fallen afoul of hard times. That is misfortune indeed. It has steadily built a name for achievement in organic gardening and practical applications of agricultural theory. But there are bright spots. The buyer, for three hundred and twenty-five thousand dollars is a New Alchemy offspring. The Cape Cohousing Committee's ten member families propose to construct a cooperative village on the Institute's twelve acres. It means that the site will remain protected from commercial and residential growth. New Alchemy's history and high purpose commend the Institute unmistakably to the Cape's community concern."

Judy's next and far more painful task was to communicate the news in more detail to New Alchemy's members and friends. A draft of her letter, dated mid-June, read in part: "If you have seen the enclosed newspaper [*Cape Cod Times*] article, you will know that the land and buildings at the Institute are being sold. The good news is that the new owners of the site and facilities include and are being inspired by some of the longest running New Alchemists. The important P.S. to this is that New Alchemy is not closing. We hope to continue our contacts with you and to facilitate the start-up of a renewed New Alchemy when the time is right."

It was true that many people, perhaps the majority, agreed with Judy that some kind of "Project Phoenix" could still arise from the ashes. I was not one of them. I was convinced that the New Alchemy story in that incarnation was over. We had been blessed with an ideal resolution to a heartbreaking dilemma. Having been granted a dignified exit, I had enough survival instinct not to milk the curtain calls. In this I was something of a lone voice. The one idea that I could happily support, as did everyone else, was that the gardens be used for community-supported agriculture (CSA).

The CSA venture proved successful and encouraged some of the staff to petition the board to consider the creation of what they called a new New Alchemy. My response was a sinking feeling. I was among the strongest advocates of bringing the Institute to an honorable closure. My primary reason was financial. We had always accepted economic insecurity as the price of doing what we wanted to do. But destitution loomed, and there were no solutions anywhere on the horizon. Less tangibly, I felt the magic was gone—that whatever it is that brings individuals together with their moment in time to create an entity larger than the sum of the parts, or of their individual lives. For the last few years New Alchemy had felt like a wraith of its former self. Once we had achieved closure with Cape Cohousing, it seemed to me it was most appropriate to let the existing Institute be claimed by the past, as many people already felt it had been. Most important, I felt the alchemy would continue on the land itself, loved and cared for by some of the people who knew it best.

After all we had been through, the final closure was, for me, almost anticlimatic. I was the only person who had been part of the New Alchemy story—albeit with wildly oscillating levels of participation—from beginning to end. I was there from the moment John said, "New Alchemy?" to deciding that "the noble thing to do was to close the New Alchemy chapter of history." The institutional story, for me, was complete as it stood. I was convinced that we had explored all the options and found none to be viable. New Alchemy had been in intensive care with inadequate life support for too long. By that time most of my fellow board members agreed with me. Once more the board collectively played the heavy and turned down the staff's proposal. We signed a letter to this effect, dated November 1, 1991.

It said in part, "It is clear to us that the Institute has in recent years lacked the inspired leadership that could enunciate a vision and galvanize a group of talented researchers and educators to translate that vision into a unified and coherent program. It is equally clear that the foundering condition we have been in during this time is well known and that, despite the vacuum, no leadership has come forth to restore the effectiveness of our activities, to say nothing of the magic. Signals from the funding community indicate that significant support is neither available nor on the horizon. It is our conviction that the energy that would have to be expended revitalizing a badly wounded organization would be more productively applied in other ways."

Needless to say it was not a popular decision. A letter from a former staff member who had been deeply committed to making another try no doubt spoke for many others. She wrote, "How cruel to decide among yourselves that this 'wounded organization' is not worth reviving. This decision, as many others, should not have been made by the board in isolation. Whatever else, I hope that we can each learn something from its demise so that we will be less likely, if given the possibility, to lose such a treasure again." It was pointless to reiterate that we were as unhappy as she was; that the existing structure and relationship of the Institute and board had emerged from its own restructuring process. We had explored all the options, but we were nonetheless miserable about how our decisions affected the staff and deeply disliked being in that position.

With the sale of the land and buildings to Cape Cohousing/the Green Center (now called Alchemy Farm), the board was able to pay all the bills and meet all the Institute's financial obligations. In the hope of making a strategic difference in their work, we donated all remaining funds to two spin-off nonprofit organizations, Bill McLarney's ANAI in Costa Rica and the Cape and Islands' Self Reliance Coalition. The final piece of business for the board was deciding to whom we should pass on the tax-exempt, not for profit (501-C3) status of the Institute. We were unanimous in our decision that the nonprofit status and number should be inherited by Cohousing. I remain convinced that we had no choice but to act as we did, and that closing down New Alchemy and giving Cape Cohousing free reign with the future of the site was by far the happiest ending we could have devised.

In June 1992 the board drafted and dispatched its final communiqué: "There is no softening the hard fact that this is the final communication you will receive from the New Alchemy Institute—under that name. After many months of extremely painful deliberation, the board decided that the optimism we felt a year ago about keeping the Institute going until we could rise from the ashes was misplaced, and that the noble thing to do was to close the New Alchemy chapter of history. The name the New Alchemy Institute will be given back to John and Nancy Jack Todd. The non-profit organization cohousing group, with The Green Center as its working name, will live on at the site. New Alchemy's library will soon be reshelved and reopened for public use. The Institute's records are being deposited in the American Archives of Agriculture at Iowa State University."

As J. Baldwin later pointed out, New Alchemy had already exhibited a remarkable longevity. "In contrast to most groups," he recalled, "NAI was based on disciplined science. Research results were eligible to be taken seriously in high places (though rather later than one would hope) and interns could earn academic credit—an effective way to breed protégés who will someday further the work. I felt best when working with a congenial team wherein members temporarily shed egos to explore some mysterious aspect of Universe works, and then apply that knowledge. It is the only way I know to bring the fierce joy with *knowing* I am doing what I have been built to do—especially when it brings success. I'll bet I'm not the only Alchie worker bee who reveled and grew in the exuberant seethe that nurtured and rewarded sharp thinking, hard work, and risk. What we discovered and demonstrated at NAI is becoming mainstream at last, though we do seem to be a bit short on credits. 'Twas ever thus. Ain't seen many opportunities like that before or since. No regrets—I'd gladly try it again."

There was no question that it was the financial crisis that was the primary cause for closing New Alchemy, but it was not the only reason. As we all came to realize, we were no longer offering anything sufficiently unique or cutting edge to compete for adequate outside support. There was also, after Greg's departure, a creativity vacuum that bred in turn a lack of excitement. The Institute was still on the side of what Zen poet Gary Snyder had called "the transforming energy." But it was no longer generating it. There had been a shift from inner purpose and necessity to responding to perceived needs. J. Baldwin had his take on this as well. "We also learned that experimental institutions ride a wave," he recalled. "The enterprise is born and grows strong seeking and celebrating its ideal form and goals, and exploring its limits. Unless injected from time to time with the energy that accompanies new and daring attempts, it matures and eventually poops out." Somehow the long process of the transition from the poetic to the purely practical, from serving as center of inspiration to becoming a source of information, however useful, had robbed New Alchemy of its uniqueness—its alchemy. It was the fire that ignited an institute, but ultimately it eluded being institutionalized.

What was most important about New Alchemy, and will remain so, was that it was the birthplace and incubator for ideas that are the building blocks for sustainable and lasting cultures. We had, in our experiments in applied Gaia, decoded some of the elements for healing both people and the planet and had helped to give the world what Gregory Bateson had called a "paradigm with a future." The seeds and the thought forms that we planted and so carefully tended at New Alchemy continue to spread and take root. And the irreplaceable memories will always be there for us. Kate Eldred recalled, "We know that it was never quite as golden and united as we remember, but it was there . . . those moments when the interns and the children were playing under the mulberry tree, the harvest was coming in hugely, dogs were running and barking, and we were saving the world as a community."

chapter ten

Ocean Arks: Restoring the Water

The moving waters at their priest-like task
Of pure ablution round Earth's human shores.
—John Keats, "Bright Star"

The winding down of New Alchemy, hard as it was to swallow, represented neither an end nor a negation of all that had taken place in the twenty-year life of the Institute. Its closing, in retrospect, was more analogous to the bursting of a seedpod, the fruits of which scattered far and wide to take many forms over the course of time. Alchemy Farm, as the cohousing community started by Earle Barnhart and Hilde Maingay is now called, lives on at the site, a once and future testimonial to New Alchemy and its ideas. In terms of the application and extension of the research, however, Ocean Arks International is the direct heir.

The beginnings of Ocean Arks go back to December 1976 when John Todd and I were invited to a combined celebration and brainstorming session to honor the seventy-fifth birthday of anthropologist Margaret Mead. An intermittent partnership with Dr. Mead emerged from that meeting, and she was to have a profound influence on the direction of our work for many years. A few months after our meeting, Dr. Mead invited us to join her as part of the American Delegation to the Pacific Science Congress on Appropriate Technology on the island of Bali in Indonesia. People rarely if ever said no to Dr. Mead, so in the middle of the whirlwind New Alchemy summer of 1977, John and I broke with our custom of staying close to home base and allowed ourselves to be drawn away for a few weeks

We spent some time with Dr. Mead on Java prior to the conference, which gave the three of us time to adapt to one another, and we became a companionable trio that was part mentor/students, part working colleagues, and part quasi-family. We found ourselves enthralled by her stories of the countless adventures, discoveries, anomalies, and friendships of her long career. After I suggested to John that he couch any of his ideas in the form of a question rather than a statement, the forceful Dr. Mead became much more receptive to his thinking. "John Todd doesn't have a lot of ideological rubbish in his head," she later claimed. "He doesn't demean high technology but uses the best of it. He can consider and deal with a large number of variables and his holistic thinking is crucial."

At one point during our time in Java, John and I were taken to see a farm near the city of Bandung. For John it was a once-in-a-lifetime experience. After years of seeking as we roamed rural areas in Canada, the States, Costa Rica, England, and France, seeing parts but never the whole in terms of the integration he sought, he came upon it at last in the highlands of Indonesia. Dodging local people leading produce-laden donkeys as we approached, he was confronted not with the theory but with the practice of a thousand years of stewardship, a time-tested traditional model of the integration we had been evolving at New Alchemy. John later wrote, "All the major types of agriculture had been interwoven and balanced on one piece of land. There were trees, livestock, grains, grasses, vegetables, and fish, but no single one was allowed to dominate. As significant as the disparate elements were the connecting relationships between and among water and aquaculture, land and agriculture. The native forest had been replaced by domestic food-bearing trees that prevented erosion of the hillsides. Water entered the farm in a relatively pure state through a ditch that ran along the contours of the land. To charge it with nutrients to fertilize as well as irrigate the crops, it flowed directly beneath the animal sheds and the household latrine. The manure-enriched water was subsequently aerated by passing over a small waterfall. It was then directed into deep channels between crops being grown in raised beds. It did not splash onto the plants but seeped laterally into the soil. In this way animal and human wastes were put to good use as fertilizers but pathogen contamination of the crops was minimized. The gardens filtered and, to a degree, purified the water."

"Any water that had not been absorbed in the garden was rechanneled to flow into small ponds where fish were hatched and raised. Plants like sweet potatoes and manioc or taro that grow from tubers rimmed the banks of the aquaculture ponds. The leaves were used as mulch or fed to the fish. The tubers were consumed by the people and chopped for their livestock. From the fishponds the water, once again enriched, flowed into rice paddies, flooding and fertilizing them. The nutrient and purification cycle was repeated as the rice absorbed nu-

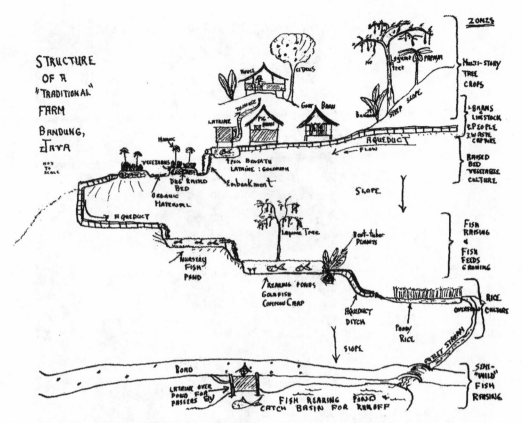

John's schematic of the farm on Java.

trients and organic materials. At the bottom reaches of the farm the water entered a large communal pond. From time to time the farmers drained the pond and hauled the sediments and organic materials back up the hill to maintain the fertility of the higher growing areas." John was deeply impressed at the exacting degree to which farmers had worked out the relationships of balanced interdependence between the various components. The levels of nutrient recycling and the integration of husbandry, rice culture, poultry, and fish and vegetable production were more sophisticated than any he had known. Nowhere else had he seen farming techniques that prevented soil fertility from deteriorating year after year, century after century.

When we moved on to Bali, in the times we were free to explore, I encountered a way of life that held comparable significance for me. Dr. Mead made a point of showing us something we had only glimpsed in books or the occasional film: a culture that was not yet fragmented. Religion, a modified form of Hinduism, was central to all of life. Not only the ordering of work and festival days and agricultural practices but the omnipresent arts and crafts and the very rich artistic life were part of an age-old, spiritually based way of life. Fresh flowers were placed on altars and at sacred places in temples and household shrines every morning.

Balinese river guardian.

Music, drama, and dance, springing from religious observations, were interwoven with daily life and were performed, not by professional groups, but by the villagers themselves. There was no division between sacred and secular; they formed a seamless whole. The painting, sculpture, and crafts rivaled the performing arts in aesthetics and technique. Almost everything on Bali was beautiful. Villages and houses were tended and cared for under the guardianship of omnipresent images of the gods and goddesses. Conflicting demands of religion and economic contingencies did not shatter the continuity of life there. People were not torn. It was this seamless integration of the sacred and the continuity with mindscape and landscape that Dr. Mead wanted us to understand as basic to Balinese life and which had maintained continuity and stability for more than a thousand years.

After we left Bali, we met once more with Dr. Mead before she died. She was anxious that the New Alchemy paradigm of providing for basic human needs and creating sustainable technologies be made available in developing countries before they committed themselves irrevocably to the path of industrialization. Although less discussed at that time, the trend toward corporate domination of the global economy was gaining momentum. It was clear that disadvantaged people everywhere would only become more so. One of the ideas we discussed then was that of a "Biological Hope Ship."

Dr. Mead's directive led John to wonder if it might be possible to set the New Alchemy Ark afloat—literally. What if we could design and build a sail-powered, greenhouse-bearing, transport vessel? The ship would both grow and carry materials such as seeds, plants, trees, and fish to impoverished areas, bringing biological resources—carefully selected to try to avoid introducing exotic or invasive species—that could be used to restore depleted ecosystems. This was the origin of the idea of the Ocean Ark and the eponymous source of our next nonprofit organization. But, like the Ark on Prince Edward Island, our seagoing Ark proved to be an idea well ahead of its time. Design for a twenty-first century Ocean Ark began in November 2004. Nonetheless, it was John's pondering the concept of a sailing bioshelter that spawned a second project. This involved building a fleet of sail-powered, state-of-the-art work boats intended to free coastal peoples from dependency on foreign oil and spare parts for motors. In this phase, sponsored by the Canadian International Development Agency, we got as far as designing, building, and testing a prototype sail-powered trimaran. We called it the "ocean pickup" because we wanted it to be associated with the reliable utilitarian virtues of its four-wheeled predecessor. Again the world proved not ready for the idea of, in this case, switching from outboard motors to sail. It did afford John, our son Jonathan, and some of their saltier seagoing colleagues many, sometimes hair-raising, adventures testing the boat with fishermen in Guyana and Costa Rica.

Sadly, then as now, not many people saw either floating bioshelters or sail-powered work boats as priorities. So, with his mind once again onshore, John began to consider applying his knowledge of aquatic ecosystems to water chemistry and water remediation. Maintaining water quality had been fundamental to raising record crops of fish and was a major focus of New Alchemy's National Science Foundation–sponsored research. By this time, the late 1980s, the widespread deterioration of water quality was piquing public interest. Many people, ourselves included, were concluding that our local water was not safe to drink. On Cape Cod many people were attributing the growing prevalence of cancer to the military, industrial, household, and agricultural chemicals and pollutants being discarded down drains to end up in our groundwater. Cape Cod's groundwater is contained in a single-source aquifer in the form of a widespread lens that lies just 20 feet below the surface of the land. Rain and snow trickling through the sandy soil are the only sources for recharging the aquifer. Clearly, Cape Cod had a water problem, and John was determined to tackle it. He was upset not so much at

The ocean pickup, the *Edith Muma*, off the west coast of Costa Rica.

having to buy drinking water as with the callous despoliation of a resource fundamental to life itself.

Fortunately, we had already established an organizational form for him to do so. Thanks to our adventures in trying to launch an Ocean Ark and the ocean pickup, John and I had founded our second institute. Ocean Arks International was officially incorporated as a nonprofit on December 21, 1981, and was the hat we wore in the years we were fund-raising, building, sailing, and promoting our seagoing ventures. Although the name was a bit ambiguous when we switched our focus to water remediation, Ocean Arks was by then sufficiently well known that we felt another identity change might be more confusing than helpful and we stuck with it. Over the years the basic mission and guiding principle of Ocean Arks International has been, in John's words, to serve the needs of the water.

Unexpectedly, Ocean Arks' first opportunity for working with contaminated water came not on the Cape but at the Sugarbush ski resort in Vermont. In 1986 some of the people in the town of Warren, located directly below the resort, were worried about the possibility of spills of the chlorine gas that was being used to treat the Sugarbush wastewater. This led John to speculate on the feasibility of reducing or eliminating chlorine from the treatment process. The management of the resort proved open to alternative ideas for treating their wastewater. The upshot was a chance for Ocean Arks to design and build a prototype treatment plant and to apply variations on New Alchemy/NSF water management to a real-life situation. An Ocean Arks crew designed and built the system in a matter of months. The Sugarbush water reclamation system took the familiar and well-tried form of a bioshelter containing an enclosed ecosystem. With a 15,000-gallon capacity, it was designed to treat the equivalent of about ten households. Inside the structure the water being treated was directed through a series of intercon-nected, ground-level raceways that culminated in a planted, artificial marsh for the final polishing. To demonstrate the quality of the treated effluent, we grew trout in a large, attached outdoor tank.

Time was on our side for a while. The Sugarbush plant became operational in the spring, a time of year when treating sewage and wastewater from a ski resort in a solar-powered plant did not present an undue challenge. The sun was high in the sky, and the load was light enough to give the contained ecosystems time to establish themselves and to develop biological diversity. By summer it was transforming wastewater into a high-quality, advanced treated effluent. John ex-plained: "We are experimenting with a method of treating water and sewage based on the natural purifying powers of aquatic ecosystems provided with ad-ditional air. The wastewater is directed into a slow flowing channel, which me-anders through a solar greenhouse and terminates in a wetland. Bacteria, algae, microscopic animals, snails, fish, and higher plants rafted on the water surface can completely transform sewage into food chains and high quality water."

The easy stage was over when winter approached. The plant then was charged with processing the results of a population explosion of skiers at a time of year when the sun slipped behind the hills at just after two o'clock in the afternoon and temperatures hovered around zero degree Fahrenheit. The BOD (biological oxygen demand), as they say in the treatment trade, was extremely high and the capacity of the biological systems to remove nitrogen, particularly in the form of toxic ammonia, was decidedly challenged. But our contained ecosystem rallied and proved, as James Lovelock had once said of the natural world, "a little like a Victorian grandmother—tougher than one would have thought!" Not only did the biota remove almost 99 percent of the ammonia, but they absorbed sludge to a degree that aroused suspicion among regulatory authorities. They demanded we drain the ecosystem to determine exactly what had happened. When we

Water being treated in
the channel at Sugarbush.

complied, only the smallest amount of sludge could be detected. The rest had been digested by the microorganisms. Faith in the metabolic capacity of John's biological consortium was either established or exonerated. We reinstalled the living systems and the Sugarbush plant was pronounced a success.

Donella Meadows devoted one of her weekly newspaper columns to the story. "The Sugarbush treatment plant is an arched, transparent plastic greenhouse," she wrote. "Inside, under a network of walkways, is a greenish pool with air bubbling through it. The pool is made up of sewage effluent, but the place smells good, like a greenhouse, humid and fertile. At the far end is a lush growth of plants—bamboo and cattails and swamp irises. The workers from the resort come in here to sunbathe during their lunch hour."

John further explained: "The Sugarbush facility represents a new direction in wastewater treatment. It depends upon sunlight and photosynthesis for its primary energy source, avoids the use of hazardous treatment chemicals and, finally, breaks ranks with the wastewater industry by not separating the solids from the liquid portion of the waste. We do not add chemicals like aluminum salts to produce two separate waste streams in the form of sludges and supernatents. The whole waste stream is kept in suspension and integrated into ecological food chains. The end products are fish, flowers, trees, and clean water. The system has the natural purifying cycles of a lake or stream, but the processes are much faster than those occurring in nature."

With this success at Sugarbush our newly land-based Ocean Arks seemed to be finding its organizational niche. By this time there was more going on than could be coordinated out of our house, as we had been doing until then, and we rented an office in Falmouth to serve as our administrative center. We had a staff of three holding the fort there, with several volunteers and part-time people coming and going between Vermont and a new Cape-based bioremediation project. Since then, and until 2003, Ocean Arks has been a mainly project-oriented organization, analogous in some ways to a consulting or architectural firm. We did not advertise or seek market opportunities but were active in connecting with civic and commercial organizations needing advice on their use of water. We tackled problems in water remediation as they presented themselves, which, given the number of problems with water, brought a considerable amount of work our way. Unlike New Alchemy's much broader agenda, we did not conceptualize Ocean Arks as an incubator of social change. Many of the issues that we had struggled for earlier, like equality for women and minimal hierarchy, by then were taken for granted, at least in our circles. And most of our best engineers were women.

As had happened at New Alchemy, however, the law governing the conduct of nonprofit organizations—as well as our own inclination—mandated that we keep supporters informed of the work as Ocean Arks unfolded. Once again a newsletter of some kind was in order. The skills most in demand for the Ocean Arks mission involved training in biology, engineering, administration, and fundraising, none of which was my strong suit, but a newsletter was my sort of thing. My second publishing effort, Ocean Arks' *Annals of Earth Stewardship,* was meatier than a newsletter and more like a newspaper in style—a sort of scientific/literary tabloid. In the first issue I explained, "*Annals of Earth Stewardship* seeks, through written communication, to disseminate the ideas and practice of ecological sustainability throughout the world."

Predictably, I loved putting *Annals* together. It gave me freedom and a chance to research issues that most interested me and to write exactly what I thought. Many former New Alchemists and other friends and colleagues, including Donella Meadows, David Orr, and Wes Jackson, contributed. And once or twice I have pulled off a real scoop. In late October 1983, for example, George Woodwell, the founder and director of the prestigious Woods Hole Research Center, chaired an international scientific conference called "The Long-Term, Worldwide Biological Consequences of Nuclear War." The scientists attending presented evidence that even a limited nuclear exchange would trigger what they called a nuclear winter that would imperil most of life on Earth. Although the *New Yorker* commented, "It would have been appropriate if every newspaper in the world had turned over its entire front page to headlines announcing the conference's findings," the meeting received very little media coverage. I interviewed Dr. Woodwell for the next *Annals*. He explained concisely the mutually suicidal potential of even a limited use of the nuclear arsenal. As an editor I felt very smug about carrying a report that not only had largely been bypassed by the media but beat the cutting-edge *CoEvolution Quarterly* to the punch.

The lengthy appellation—the *Annals of Earth Stewardship*—however, was proving too much for most people to get their tongues around. Two years after the first issue appeared, William Irwin Thompson of the Lindisfarne Association, a brilliant, multidisciplinary association of individuals dedicated to fostering the emergence of a new global culture, suggested we combine the *Annals of Earth Stewardship* with his *Lindisfarne Letter* and issue a joint publication. We seized the moment of collaboration to shorten the title to *Annals of Earth*. I remained editor, and Bill signed on as contributing editor. We rolled off the press three times a year. Bill and his Lindisfarne connections gave *Annals* an extended intellectual rigor and a wider philosophical scope, and together we ranged far and wide over the fields of applied ecology and cultural change. The partnership continued until Bill retired from Lindisfarne in 1997. *Annals of Earth* is still the voice of Ocean Arks.

Doing Good Things in Bad Places

The next great leap forward in applying New Alchemy–derived aquatic ecosystems to restoring polluted water came in 1988 in response to an appeal from the Cape Cod town of Harwich. The Sugarbush experiment paled beside the task that Ocean Arks would confront in Harwich, making our habitual tilting at windmills seem eminently sane. Our work at Sugarbush was well known in Harwich, thanks to a site visit by town officials instigated by local resident Hunter Craig. A craggy ex-Marine and World War II pilot, Hunter loved Cape Cod—he called it his girlfriend. But unlike many of us who profess to love the Cape, Hunter was determined to do everything he could to save it.

Harwich was faced with a nasty problem. Like the rest of the Cape, it had no sewer system as such. The wastes and sewage from households and commercial and public buildings drained into septic tanks. These tanks occasionally had to be emptied. This process entailed pumping the residue, called septage, into tank

The Harwich septage lagoon with the Eco-Machine just installed.

trucks and conveying it to a disposal area. Septage is forty to a hundred times more concentrated than sewage. In the case of Harwich—and a number of other towns—septage was then pumped into an open holding pond, or septage lagoon.

The septage lagoon at Harwich was unarguably the most disgusting thing I have ever seen. It was hideously repugnant. In attempting to explain it to *Annals* readers, I used descriptions from Dante's *Inferno*: "The banks were crusted over with a mould from the vapour below, which concretes upon them, which does battle with the eyes and nose." And "dipped in excrement as it had flowed from human privies." He could hardy have been more accurate. The slimy black surface of that pond embodied to me Jung's concept of the shadow: the unrecognized and repressed side of our collective behavior made manifest.

The lagoon sat in sandy porous soil, 20 to 25 feet directly over the same water table that was the public source of drinking water. The Massachusetts Department of Environmental Protection had ordered the town to treat the septage. Hunter Craig urged a variation on the Sugarbush experiment. The end result was that Ocean Arks and the Town of Harwich agreed to a pioneering experiment. The people of Harwich, bolstered by a grant from the Massachusetts Center for Excellence, voted the funds for us to design, build, and operate a prototype living system to treat the septage as it came from the trucks. To our knowledge it had never been done before. The Harwich disposal area became Ocean Arks' next venue.

The landscape—and subsequently the mindscape there—rapidly underwent a dramatic change. Granted, on entering the gate, the difference was not immediately apparent. There were the usual heaps of refuse, mounds of gravelly landfill, blowing litter, and rapacious seagulls, and to the left lay the fetid septage lagoons. But shortly after the arrival of the Ocean Arks crew that summer, there rose, on the far side of the ponds, a stately line of twenty-one, 5-foot-tall translucent cylinders—the familiar New Alchemy solar-algae ponds. The tanks were linked like beads on a string and aerated through plastic tubing. On the surface water of each tank floated a small raft that supported different combinations of floating plants and a few small trees. The septage passed through each tank in turn until it reached the last, a process that took twelve days. From the last tank it was drained into a long, waist-high wooden trough that ran the length of the entire row. We lined the trough with plastic and filled it with aquatic plants and organisms. Its function was to serve as an analogue of a marsh in nature and was intended to do the final polishing or purifying of the septage. From the simulated marsh the treated liquid was discharged into the nearest lagoon.

The apparent simplicity of the design, which we called the Eco-Machine, made a dramatic and graphic impression on visitors who, mainly by word of mouth, heard of the experiment and flocked to see it. You could see the sludge being fed into the first tank: thick, wretched, contaminated, and black. You could then follow the progressive clarity of the water as it made its way along the length of the tanks and through the course of the simulated marsh. The only visible participants in the transformation were air bubbles, floating plants, the occasional snail, and, in the last tank, a small cluster of fish. The clear water at the end was visible testimony to the fact that natural systems are incomparable recyclers.

In the less visible realm the transformation was even more dramatic. Before treatment began, independent laboratory tests had shown the sludge to contain fourteen volatile organic compounds that are listed as carcinogenic by the U.S. Environmental Protection Agency (EPA). Three of them—toluene, methylene chloride, and trichloroethane—were in very high concentration. After passing through our system, independent tests indicated that 99 percent of the ammonia and phosphorous had been removed. Over the four-month trial period, thirteen of the carcinogenic compounds were completely eliminated. The toluene was 99.9 percent removed. Nitrate levels being discharged were down to one-tenth of those considered safe for well water. The treated effluent was of a higher quality than required by EPA standards. We subsequently have found that the costs of installing such a system, or any living technology, is generally equivalent to standard treatment, but it has no need for expensive and dangerous chemicals. Its ability to self-organize and self-repair reduces costs significantly over time.

The Harwich Eco-Machine with parallel marsh.

These results came as an epiphany for John. Once again the plants and animals—and his combination of biological knowledge and intuitive understanding of healing—had seen him through. At Harwich he demonstrated conclusively that ecologically designed systems could treat not only sewage but septage. This was crucial to giving him the confidence that he could devise systems to cope with some of the worst pollution problems facing humanity. The natural systems at the Harwich lagoon had given a high-profile and irrefutable demonstration of their innate ability to self-design, heal, and self-repair on their own. With a little engineering and astute application by attuned human participants, we now know that these systems can help us undo much of the damage done to the waters of the planet. Harwich proved to John that, as he said at the time, "You can do good things in bad places." He later explained, "Gaia knows what she is doing, and our best bet is to get better at playing junior partner in the overall scheme of things."

I had an epiphany of my own one afternoon as I gazed at the row of familiar solar-algae tanks standing fortress-like across the pond from me. I thought of all the billions of dollars spent every year on military hardware. Yet there, in the inauspicious setting of the Harwich disposal area, it was obvious that humanity's ultimate line of defense lay in the sun-powered, microbe-based ecosystems that are part of and contiguous with Earth's living systems—of which we are not apart, but a part. John was right. Gaia does know what she is doing.

Rafted plants on the water surface of the Harwich Eco-Machine.

After several more years of research and testing on our part, Ocean Arks' eco-logical water treatment system was officially certified by the Commonwealth of Massachusetts in 1992. Achieving the first state certification to bestow legitimacy on processes that had been operational on the planet for several billion years was one of Ocean Arks' hardest-won battles. At one point John was both fined and re-warded by the government in the same week. The local press followed the story with keen interest. The *Cape Cod Times* for July 9, 1989, reported: "It's been a roller coaster week for John Todd. On Tuesday he was lumped in with a group of alleged scofflaws, targeted by the state for pollution. And yesterday he received a letter informing him he was selected for the first Chico Mendes Memorial Award for en-vironmental merit from the federal Environmental Protection Agency." The *Times* editorialized, "When it comes to scientific and financial efficiencies, Dr. Todd ap-pears to win the contest hands down." The *Falmouth Enterprise* agreed. Under the heading "Bureaucracy Triumphant," it reported: "The state's five thousand dollar fine was a triumph of bureaucracy. Dr Todd had somehow failed, in constructing a facility for the treatment of sewage, to fill out all of the forms. The plant worked. It is an important advance in waste treatment." As John had explained at the time, "The problems lay in the fact that we were taking our instructions from Boston or the head office and the regional office overreacted to the slight." Trailing this dubious distinction John accepted his award, battled the fine, and, after several years, finally won.

Beyond Harwich

With the fine still hanging in the balance, John was nonetheless ready to move on to another chance to test his still controversial approach for tackling pollution problems. The next overture came from Providence, Rhode Island, prompted by citizens anxious to protect Narragansett Bay. There we were challenged to see if our systems could treat the wastes of an industrial city. Among the industrial effluents were heavy metals from the city's many jewelry makers.

Because of the complicated engineering involved, John joined forces with the peripatetic Scottish engineer Michael Shaw. Theirs was to prove as long-lived and fruitful a partnership as John's collaboration with Bill McLarney. As wildly idealistic as John and equally dedicated, Michael balanced John's biological creativity with a strong background in ecological engineering—a symbiosis that has proved indispensable to their many subsequent projects. Following their designs, Ocean Arks built a greenhouse at Fields Point in Providence, adjacent to the city's main waste treatment facility. Although working at the Harwich dump had somewhat inured us to unlovely settings, the proximity to Providence's municipal dog pound amid the dregs of the city made trying to create another symbol of transformation truly daunting. But once the greenhouse was up, the same old alchemy slowly took over.

The design for the contained ecosystems called for four parallel treatment systems—four long rows of the ever-adaptable solar-algae ponds linked together for the length of each of the lines. The tanks that handled the strongest incoming waste were kept in a room closed to visitors. The dominant life-forms at this stage were the microbial and algal communities and water hyacinth. In an adjacent large, airy greenhouse that was open to the public, each treatment line flowed into two gravel bed marshes. These were planted with wetland species, predominantly bulrushes. The marshes were drained periodically to simulate the cycles of a tidal marsh. From the marshes the flow was pumped back up into another series of tanks bearing temperate and tropical plants on floating racks. The animal population was made up of zooplankton, snails, minnows, bivalve mussels, and hybrid striped bass. After the flow passed through a biofilter, the final cleansing took place in another marsh encased in a metal trough. The effluent was directed into it through polished, art deco water faucets. The general effect was to strike a

The Providence Eco-Machine from the entrance.

metallic, gleaming note in the middle of the rioting biological systems once they became established. John intended the marked contrast as something of a joke, and most people loved it. Some of the engineers and regulators, however, found such levity inappropriate to the serious business of sewage treatment.

Although the plant was far from fully operational, after the inevitable work blitz to meet our deadline, we opened it with a great flurry in July 1988. On a perfect summer afternoon city dignitaries, representatives of the Narragansett Bay Commission, Ocean Arkers, business associates, friends, and an unexpected delegation from Japan, all dressed to the nines, assembled at our small oasis. Sea breezes ruffled banners, flags flew, a jazz band played, young plants added a hopeful green to the dreary landscape, and the flowers that we had hastily put in and coaxed into bloom blazed brightly. It was all a bit incongruous in the middle of the surrounding wasteland, but no one seemed to mind. Visitors toured the plant,

Joan Wilder of Ocean Arks inside the Providence plant.

sweating profusely in the tropical environment, and emerged intrigued with this exotic approach to waste treatment. The vitality of the natural world was palpable.

How well the plant would perform was still unknown, but by then we were much more confident of its—and our—abilities to, as John described it, "bring nature, science, architecture and art together to serve the water." Scientists from Rhode Island and Brown Universities, the Massachusetts Institute of Technology, and the Woods Hole Oceanographic Institution collaborated with Ocean Arks in the research. Over the next several years the Providence plant more than rose to the challenge. Toxins were absorbed and heavy metals were sequestered by the biological systems. Once the plant became operational, the discharge more than met the heavy metal standards for drinking water. We had anticipated the digestion of the toxins, but we considered the sequestering of the heavy metals another breakthrough. Based on his knowledge of research at the Max Planck Institute, which had demonstrated the ability of certain plants, particularly *Scirpus*, or bulrush, to sequester heavy metals, John had planted them in the marshes. His results corroborated the earlier data from Max Planck. Heavy metals were sequestered in the plants and also onto filamentous algae communities on the walls of the tanks. The metals were removed by harvesting the plants and algae.

In a variation on his breakthrough at Harwich, John again found inspiration at Providence. Late one afternoon, feeling down for some reason (most likely, he thinks, perennial fiscal shortfall), he stopped by the plant alone. Stepping inside the greenhouse he was, in his words, "immediately engulfed by the sight and sounds of cascading water and the exuberant botany, the lushness of the plants, and the vitality of the other life forms invisibly playing their part in their small ecosystem. Fish were breeding under mats of floating aquatic plants. An Asian wind chime sounded." As the tension began to flood from him, he had a flash—another Aha!—that such intentional ecologies might some day play a role in healing people as well as in restoring water.

As our systems continued to prove themselves, we felt compelled to seize every chance we could to demonstrate the Ocean Arks ecosystems approach to treating wastes. So when the town of Marion, Massachusetts, directly across Buzzard's Bay from our favorite Cape Cod beaches, asked whether we could treat boat wastes, knowing wastes pumped out of boats to be a major source of marine pollution, we again agreed to try. Once the Providence plant was up and running, we began work in Marion. Again our venue was the town sewage treatment plant, adjacent to the dump. But there, instead of neglected or dying dogs, our nonhuman co-inhabitants on the site were a friendly mix of geese and goats, guarded by a watchful llama. It was definitely a more upbeat work neighborhood. The innovative element at Marion was the incorporation of marine organisms such as salt marsh hay into the bioremedial process. And again we demonstrated the underlying axiom of ecological design. Waste is a resource out of place, and the right combination of organisms can neutralize substances that, when left untreated, remain toxins.

With these projects Ocean Arks was establishing a pattern that was to see us through the next decade. We were starting to design and build contained ecosystems to restore water that had been subjected to many different types of contamination. Some were small prototypes, intended to demonstrate the viability of the technology. Then, when a commercial client, most frequently an industry such as food processing or a brewery, decided to install one of our systems, we would build a full-scale plant, train personnel in maintenance, and turn the management over to them. When the client was a community or town, as was the case in Harwich and Marion, we would work cooperatively with local people and remain more involved. Crisscrossing back and forth between the public and industrial spheres in this way has moved Ocean Arks applications of ecological design around the country and around the world.

chapter eleven

Ocean Arks
Sails On

I am the angel of reality
Seen for a moment standing in the door.
I am one of you and being one of you
Is being and knowing what I am and know.

Yet I am the necessary angel of Earth,
Since in my sight, you see the Earth again.
—Wallace Stevens, "Angel Surrounded by Paysans"

As the wave of innovation in water remediation gathered momentum for Ocean Arks, John Todd felt it timely that we begin to define what he was coming to call ecological design. Because, as a field of study, ecological design springs from a conscious, intimate partnering of human and evolutionary intelligence, to communicate this approach he undertook codifying the scientific information and methodologies we had accumulated to date. In writing about it, John and I had defined ecological design as "design for human settlements and infrastructures that incorporates principles inherent in the natural world in order to sustain human populations over a long span of time; adapting the wisdom and strategies of the natural world to human problems."

Ecological design is a radical departure from most current practices in that it turns to the dynamics and self-organization of almost four billion years of biological evolution and seeks to harmonize human activities within these larger flows. In his book *The Nature of Design*, David Orr described ecological design as "the careful meshing of human purposes with the larger patterns and flows of the natural world and the study of those patterns and flows to inform human actions." In their book *Ecological Design*, Sim Van der Ryn and Stuart

Cowan refer to it as "any form of design that minimizes environmentally destructive impacts by integrating itself with nature's processes."

In *Annals of Earth* John stated: "Pollution, atmospheric alteration, and the loss of soils and biotic diversity are artifacts of technological cultures estranged from the great natural systems of the planet. Modern cultures exploit the natural world and in doing so threaten their own long-term viability. It is essential that we create a truly symbiotic relationship with the natural world predicated on new highly evolved technologies. With Ocean Arks staff member Beth Josephson, John wrote a paper entitled "The Design of Living Technologies for Waste Treatment." First published in *Annals* in 1994, it subsequently appeared in the professional journal *Ecological Engineering* in 1996. In the parlance of the field, the journal announced, "This article elucidates the emerging principles required for the design of task-oriented mesocosms." In keeping with his long practice of designing to reflect the materials and processes of natural systems, John and Beth listed twelve principles fundamental to the practice of ecological design:

1. Geological and mineral diversity must be present to evolve the biological responsiveness of rich soils.

2. Nutrient reservoirs are essential to keep such essentials as nitrogen, phosphorus, and potassium available for the plants.

3. Steep gradients between subcomponents must be engineered into the system to enable the biological elements to evolve rapidly to assist in the breakdown of toxic materials.

4. High rates of exchange must be created by maximizing surface areas that house the bacteria that determine the metabolism of the system and facilitate treatment.

5. Periodic and random pulsed exchanges improve performance. Just as random perturbations foster resilience in nature, in living technologies altering water flow creates self-organization in the system.

6. Cellular design is the structural model as it is in nature where cells are the organizing unit. Expansion of a system should also use a cellular model, as in increasing the number of tanks.

7. A law of the minimum must be incorporated. At least three ecosystems such as a marsh, a pond, and a terrestrial area are needed to perform the assigned function and maintain overall stability.

8. Microbial communities must be introduced periodically from the natural world to maintain diversity and facilitate evolutionary processes.

9. Photosynthetic foundations are essential as oxygen-producing plants foster ecosystems that require less energy, aeration, and chemical management.

10. Phylogenetic diversity must be encouraged as a range of aquatic animals from the unicellular to snails to fish are as essential to the evolution and self-maintenance of the system as the plants. All five kingdoms of life must be present, as they are in the natural world; namely the bacteria, Protoctista or nucleated cells, fungi, plants, and animals.

11. Sequenced and repeated seedings are part of maintenance as a self-contained system cannot be isolated but must be interlinked through gaseous, nutrient, mineral, and biological pathways to the external environment.

12. Ecological design should reflect the macrocosmos in the microcosmos, representing the natural world miniaturized and reflecting its proportions, as in terrestrial to oceanic and aquatic areas.

This marked the peer-reviewed debut of Ocean Arks' applications of ecological design into the scientific mainstream. In less rigorously scientific circles, our so-called mesocosms were also beginning to attract the attention of the popular media. At one point *People* magazine sent a reporter to check us out. The resulting article was accompanied by a photograph taken in our kitchen at home. John and Jonathan were portrayed poring studiously over charts laid out on the counter while Susannah and I chatted in the background. The heading read, "If You Leave It to Mother Nature, Says Biologist John Todd, Sewage Doesn't Have to Go to Waste." About the same time John also made a fleeting appearance on CNN; *Garbage* magazine did a feature article; and for some inexplicable reason, the office received inquiries from *Seventeen* magazine. To bolster this outreach, we included a brief account of Ocean Arks' early work in ecological design in our book *From Eco-Cities to Living Machines: Principles of Ecological Design*.

This upsurge of interest in our work led us to expand our outreach and our mandate. Further heartened by the success at Harwich and the promising results indicated by data from the Providence and Marion facilities, John felt the need to expand OAI's collective thinking on water issues. In *Annals of Earth* he wrote, "We need to find ways to revere and protect water as the ancients did. We need to search for new ways to restore the water we have destroyed through industry and indifference." To signal our intent to the outside world, we decided to create a suborganization under the same nonprofit rubric as Ocean Arks. John continued, "This past summer we have created the Center for the Restoration of Waters at Ocean Arks International. To understand water, its chemistry, its restoration, even its sacred nature, will require many people. This is the real reason for creating the Center."

It was also the reason we decided to expand our staff and develop an education program. In the early 1990s, in addition to Beth Josephson, who managed many of the projects while producing and raising two sons, Ocean Arks expanded to include administrators Susan Peterson and Jill Ashmore; actor and journalist Joan Wilder; bright-eyed, computer-literate Karen Schwalbe; and Patrick Ryan, a young man with the right combination of intellect, idealism, and pragmatism to initiate our education and outreach programs. Our New Alchemy/Ocean Arks luck in attracting gifted, dedicated people held in all cases but one. The woman we hired as office manager and trusted to manage our finances was also very talented—unfortunately for us, her most prominent ability lay in the area of embezzling. This gift she applied ably, assisted by her former Navy Seal boyfriend, and with such skill that she was not discovered for over four years. By that time we were receiving grants from the U.S. Environmental Protection Agency, and the damage she did by manipulating several hundred thousand dollars of government funds almost ruined us. It took Ocean Arks four years to trace her paper and electronic trails and wait out the time it took for the courts to find them both guilty. She served several months in jail, but her boyfriend, an even more elusive character, managed to avoid jail time. In the meantime unflappable Megan Amsler took over the office and with stoic tolerance kept everything going as we recuperated.

In spite of the enormous setback levied by the embezzlement, Ocean Arks managed to soldier on. It was not always easy. At times we had to let good people go and scale down on programs and projects. Somehow we were able to press on with the research and the various applications of our living technologies. In 1998 when John accepted a position at the University of Vermont, we moved our main office to Burlington, and Michael Shaw replaced John as Ocean Arks' executive director. The *Annals of Earth* office stayed on the Cape.

Restorers

In the early 1990s John invented another variation on living technologies that was less directly visually traceable to the glass jars cum solar algae ponds cum contained ecosystems. It took the form of a floating unit he called a Restorer that treated polluted bodies of water such as ponds or lakes on the spot. It evolved from the next major hurdle facing Ocean Arks in terms of damaged water. It also brought us back to the scene of our 1988 breakthrough. Flax Pond has the misfortune of being located adjacent to the Harwich disposal area, not more than about a hundred yards from the ridge where the first row of solar tanks had maintained their line of defense against the pollutants in the septage lagoons. Years of seepage from the lagoons and the landfill as well as chemical run-off from nearby cranberry bogs had taken a predictable toll on the 15-acre pond. It did not have the horrifying appearance of the lagoons, but laboratory tests had revealed that it was in a very sorry state. Hydrologists confirmed that it was receiving 30 million gallons of landfill seepage a year.

Again in response to a request from the town of Harwich, Ocean Arks agreed to treat the pond. Flax Pond had been pronounced comatose. Much of the pond was virtually devoid of bottom-dwelling organisms and on the edge of what biologists call a hypertrophic state of ecological collapse. Because of high levels of coliform bacteria, toxic organic compounds, and heavy metals, it had been closed to swimming and fishing. At times in the autumn the eastern end of the pond turned red from iron-based compounds suspended in the water. Instead of being naturally digested by aquatic organisms and bacteria, organic material had accumulated and formed thick layers of sediment on the pond bottom. This created an oxygen-consuming reservoir of muck that was uninhabitable by bottom-dwelling animals. Because seepage from the landfill and the bogs was not expected to slow down in the foreseeable future, as so often happens, we had to try to initiate healing under far from ideal conditions.

In spite of all this, John felt there might be enough biological diversity left in the pond to attempt intervention. The pond, he decided, clearly needed the ministrations of a Restorer—a Pond Restorer. And that is what it got. He and Karen Schwalbe reported in *Annals*: "To begin to heal the pond we would have to expose the sediments to oxygen on a periodic basis and to create conditions that would support nitrification and sediment digestion. If we could accomplish that, the plants and animals that facilitate the self-purification metabolism of a healthy pond could reestablish themselves and help the recovery process along."

The first Pond Restorer consisted of a raft on which we mounted our old New Alchemy ally, a vertical axis Savonius rotor windmill. A shaft connected the rotors to a blade that was held suspended in the water just above the bottom of the pond. When the wind turned the rotors, the blade gently lifted the bottom water and sediments up into the oxygen-rich, sunlit waters above. When the windmills were quiet, the sediments resettled. In this way they were alternately exposed to aerobic and anaerobic conditions. With the early Restorers we also periodically pumped water-purifying bacteria and minerals down into the sediments. In spite of ongoing seepage from the lagoons, Flax Pond began to show signs of improvement not long after the Restorer was installed. After eighteen months, toxic organic compounds were no longer measurable.

John again felt his faith in natural systems had been affirmed. We had brought the pond back from the brink, but he felt we could do still better. Two years later he and Michael Shaw designed and built a second model, also for Flax Pond, which for some now forgotten reason was called Restorer One and expanded, both physically and metabolically, on the capabilities of the prototype. It consisted of a

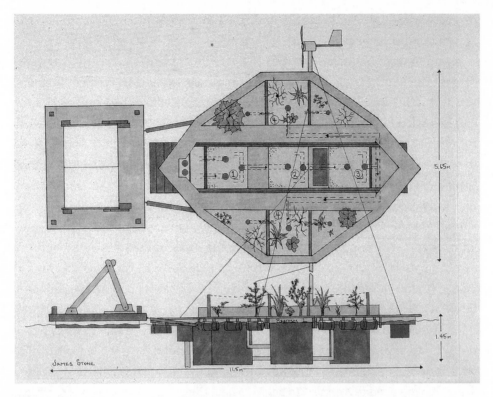

The Flax Pond Restorer. Numbers indicate the flow of water through the cells.

larger raft rimmed with a deck, which allowed for walking and workspace and enclosed nine boxlike chambers or cells. Each of these cells, like the floating environments atop the land-based systems in Harwich and Providence, contained an ecosystem intended to fulfill a specific step in the purification process. The Savonius rotor of its predecessor was replaced by a three-blade windmill and a small solar electricity–generating panel. The windmill powered airlift pumps to circulate the water through the cells. The first three cells contained semibuoyant pumice stones that supported rich microbial, algal, and animal communities such as snails and clams. The six remaining cells were filled with water-tolerant shrubs, trees, and marsh plants with roots that extended well down into the water column and provided the habitat for diverse microbial communities and refugia for zooplankton.

Two years later Restorer One had completed the healing process, and Flax Pond was officially reopened for swimming and fishing. When fish from the pond were tested in the labs at Woods Hole Oceanographic, their flesh was found to be lower in toxins and healthier than fish from other ponds in the area. John and Karen concluded their summary: "Restorers bioremediate ponds and lakes because they

Restorer One on Flax
Pond.

have the ability to initiate changes at the level of the ecosystem itself. Through altering the gaseous and food chain relationships they are able to help digest sediments, sequester metals, remove pathogens, reduce nutrient levels, diversify biota, and improve water quality."

In the late 1980s, the contained ecosystems that John had first contemplated in large jars on our front lawn, and which had been the workhorses of New Alchemy's solar aquaculture and Ocean Arks' ecological restoration, acquired a new name. One of John's business colleagues, who had been greatly impressed with their performance at Harwich, suggested we call them Living Machines. That is still the most popular, almost generic name, but it is now the corporate property of a water remediation company based in the West. We no longer use it but now refer to the name Eco-Machine. The term *Living Machine* served well, however, to explain the concepts behind the technology. John wrote at the time in *Annals*: "A Living Machine is a device made up of living organisms of all types, usually housed within a casing or structure of extremely light weight materials. Like a conventional machine it is comprised of interrelated parts with separate functions and used in the performance of some type of work. Such machines can be designed to produce fuels or food, to treat wastes, to purify air, to regulate climates or even to do all of these simultaneously. They are engineered according to the same design principles found in nature to build and regulate the ecology of forests, lakes, prairies, or estuaries. Like the planet they have hydrological and mineral cycles. They are, however, totally new contained environments."

John's report continued: "Organisms are collected from the field for these contained ecosystems and are subsequently reassembled for specific purposes. Their parts or living components can come from almost any region and be recombined in new ways. They are fundamentally different from conventional machines or biotechnologies. They represent, in essence, the intelligence of the forest or the lake reapplied to human ends. Like the forest or lake, their primary source of power is the sun. Like natural ecosystems they have the capability of self-design. They rely on biotic diversity for self-repair and protection, and for overall system efficiency. Their metabolism involves such independent qualities of life forms as replication, feeding, and waste excretion in dynamic balance with interdependent functions like gas, mineral, and nutrient exchanges. The potential contributions of such ecological engines to the twenty-first century are portentous. They require only one time use of fossil fuels in manufacture. They reintegrate wastes into larger systems and break down toxic materials or, in the case of metals, lock them up in long cycles. They have the potential to help feed people year round, especially in urban areas. Widespread implementation of these living technologies could release natural systems from bondage. By miniaturizing the footprint of essential human services they would return wild nature to its own devices and allow the restoration of large tracts of wilderness."

Developing these technologies, becoming immersed in ecological design, and applying processes derived from the natural world to human problems can be construed as what environmental writer Janine Benyus has called "biomimicry." In her acclaimed book of the same name, Benyus defines biomimicry as "a new science that studies nature's models and then imitates or takes inspiration from these designs and processes to solve human problems." She also sees biomimicry as an ecological standard by which we can judge the appropriateness of our inventions and innovations and as a mentor through which we can relearn to value rather than exploit the natural world. I have come to believe that biomimicry is at the core of what our Wampanoag friend long ago referred to as our "instructions," emerging as a result of many years of mindful attention to diverse ecosystems and the culmination of the Aha! moments this has brought.

Penetrating the Industrial World

In 2001 Ocean Arks took on its biggest project to date, involving not only Restorers on an unprecedented scale, but the largest temporary team of people we had brought together so far to design, build, and bring it to life. The client was Tyson Foods, and the focus was a wastewater lagoon for its poultry-processing plant in Berlin, Maryland, which had to be brought into compliance with EPA regulations. Heading the construction crew was our son Jonathan, who had spent his earlier career as the captain of the ocean pickup during Ocean Arks' seagoing period. His boat building and leadership experience had given him the requisite skill for the Tyson job.

The size of the wastewater lagoons and the strength of the wastes required the Tyson Restorer to be a much-scaled-up version of the original Flax Pond system. It was made up of twelve floating docks, each of them following the cellular model for ecological design, each a restorer in itself, 140 feet in length. Twenty-five species of plants totaling some twenty-five thousand plants were set into racks aligning the edges of the docks. Attached to their undersides were strips of fabric that, taken together, could be likened to an oversized version of the mops at a car wash. They served as a substrate for millions of microorganisms and whole communities of bacteria, algae, and water-filtering zooplankton.

Once the plants were installed, they attracted enthusiastic grazers from the local bird population, particularly the Canada geese, and our plant people had to rally with some elaborate netting schemes to maintain enough plant material to get the job done. The water in the open areas between the docks was treated with fine-bubble linear aerators at the bottom of the lagoon. When this jumbo Restorer was operational and proving itself, the Tyson management was more than satisfied with its still somewhat unusual treatment unit. Their effluent was brought well within state permit levels, sludge was practically eliminated, and energy efficiency improved by 74 percent. What we at Ocean Arks were most happy about was that the watershed draining into beleaguered Chesapeake Bay had been freed of a major source of contamination. Even in corporate guise, it is sometimes possible to serve the needs of the water.

The corporate sector may have monopolies in many areas, but polluted water is not one of them. In 2002 Ocean Arks took its Restorer technology to Fuzhou in southern China. The city has no sewer system. The sewage from this densely populated area, with its concentration of high-rise buildings, drains directly into an approximately 50-mile-long network of canals that wends its way through the city. Ocean Arks' first assignment was to install a prototype Restorer to decontaminate a preliminary half-mile stretch called the Baima Canal. In some ways

The Tyson Restorer.

this project harked back to the septage lagoons at Harwich in its graphic demonstration of the capabilities of the technology. Before we began work on the first stretch, it was no more than a filthy, foul-smelling trickle of water at the bottom of a cement-lined canal encasement. After a few months of work, during which the Ocean Arks crew endured heat, stench, and the unfathomable machinations of Chinese bureaucracy, they had built long rafts, installed them, and seeded them with the appropriate life-forms. As the plants grew and the root systems became established, the smell evaporated. Clear water ran through what so recently had been a disagreeable trough. The rafts were sprouting shrubs and trees, medicinal herbs, and bright flowers. Birds and butterflies not seen for years began to appear. The alchemy of healing was again transparently visible in the restored Baima Canal.

Restorers are also at work in Hawaii cleaning up contaminated water, and there are more coming online all the time. But because of its proximity to Ocean Arks' headquarters, an experimental installation in South Burlington was for more than five years regarded as the Ocean Arks flagship. Formally opened in 1997 by Vermont Senator Patrick Lahey, the facility appears from the outside to be a rather ordinary one-story greenhouse 100 feet long by 75 feet wide with an overall area of 7,500 square feet. But inside, this steamy bioshelter is literally a jungle.

Even in winter, when the deciduous willows and bald cypress trees are bare, the tropical plants remain almost alarmingly luxuriant. Ginger, philodendron,

Restorer on the
Baima Canal.

Long view of the
Baima Canal.

Life returns to the Baima Canal.

banana, elephant ear, and taro plants with trunks 2 feet in circumference and leaves 3 feet across tower overhead, grazing the translucent roof. Red, yellow, and coral cannas, hibiscus, angel's trumpet (*Brugmansia* spp.), and calla lilies the size of dinner plates bloom in their season. The plants are borne on rafts on the surface of the water in metal tanks that rise 5 feet above the concrete floor and are sunk an additional 10 feet below ground level. Sharing this watery habitat and using the plant roots as a substrate is an array of life-forms. Microscopic creatures and algae at the bottom of the food chain support the higher plants and the animals, which include gleaming Japanese koi, carp, native species of bait fish, and dignified ram's horn snails. The secret of the rampant assemblage of life here once again lies in the maximum utilization of solar energy and the rich stew of nutrients in the water on which the roots of the plants are feeding. The facility has proved its effectiveness in treating both sewage and industrial wastes to advanced water quality standards.

The struggle for acceptance of an ecosystem approach is ongoing, however. In spite of the success of Sugarbush, until recently it still was generally thought that the natural systems in the South Burlington plant would thrive in warm weather but could not weather a Vermont winter. The general consensus was that the

Entrance to the South Burlington plant.

The interior of the South Burlington plant.

Rafted plants on the water surface of the tanks in South Burlington.

water would get so cold that the ecosystems would shut down or go into a kind of hibernation. In such a state they could lose the metabolic ability to convert toxic ammonia to nitrates and nitrates to nitrogen gas. But again the resiliency of natural systems was underestimated. Because John and his colleagues seeded the ecosystems from many diverse environments, including local bodies of water in which cold-tolerant bacteria function throughout the winter, the species were able to adapt to all weathers and remained fully operational throughout the winter.

Ocean Arks' applied ecosystems are developing a secondary role as effective educators. Small classroom and desktop models are being used in classrooms in Vermont and across the country. The single most dramatic educational jolt took place in Las Vegas in 1997, where a small prototype system was treating wastes from a chocolate factory. The system had been installed on a trial basis to treat a tenth of the total waste stream. One Friday, through some combination of computer and human error, the entire waste stream was directed into our contained ecosystem. Late that afternoon the horrified operators found themselves faced with overflowing tanks of oily, fat-ridden effluent, displaced plants, and fish gasping or dying on the floor beneath them. Overwhelmed, they turned their backs, locked the doors, and went home. On Monday morning, steeled for the worst, they returned.

They were thunderstruck by what met their eyes. Granted, the dead fish had not been resurrected. But the contents of the roiling tanks had settled down and

The Las Vegas Eco-Machine.

were functioning normally. Most of the plants had settled back or could be easily righted. Just as most of us manage to recover from an excessively large dinner, the contained ecosystems had absorbed and metabolized the unexpected nutrient overload. The astonished—and relieved—engineers had only to mop the floor and compost the dead fish and plant material. Instantly won over by the efficiency of living systems, they contacted the company's administrative officers. Phone lines and e-mails hummed. Faxes flew. As a result of the unintended breakdown/breakthrough, a full-scale installation was ordered for the Las Vegas site and three more were built for affiliated food-processing plants in Texas, Brazil, and Australia. The Las Vegas engineers and administrators were complete converts. Again the merits of working with what Ron Zweig once called a pulsing, wild primordial soup—a little ecosystem piece of Gaia—had been shown to work. As it does, although less remarked upon, on an ongoing planetary scale.

There are now more than thirty comparable installations fulfilling their assigned tasks across the United States, in Canada, and around the world. Probably the best known of these is the Eco-Machine at the visitors' center at the National Audubon Center at Corkscrew Swamp in Florida. As a zero-discharge system it enables people to visit the swamp without polluting it, as wastewater is treated, sterilized, and recycled on-site. The evapotranspiration of the plants in the center's screened house, where plants and insects native to the swamp are grown, balances the liquid contributions of visitors. As these living technologies continue to prove themselves in their various functions, we hope some day to find a means to transport their restorative potential to the poorest parts of the world and attempt to prevent untold numbers of people, mainly children, from dying from waterborne diseases. In this way ecological design would truly be fulfilling its potential as a technology and a catalyst for healing.

New Levels of Integration

In 2001, Erik Wells, a young colleague and former student whose mind embraces an unusual blend of ecological awareness and business acumen, undertook a collaboration with John that could represent the most comprehensive integration of function since New Alchemy pulled food, energy, and shelter together under one roof in the Arks. The goal this time was to substantiate one of John's theories about the economic potential of integrated ecological systems. Initially called the Ocean Arks Food Group, in partnership with the city of Burlington, Vermont, and the Intervale Foundation, they are developing a year-round, agriculturally based Eco-Industrial Park. The Eco-Park, as it is usually called, is being created in incremental stages in Burlington's floodplain, known as the Intervale, which is five minutes from downtown. The businesses to be part of the mix of enterprises there include a brewery, a restaurant, several food processors, and established food growers and suppliers. We hope that one day John's ecological design studio will have a home in the form of a bioshelter there as well.

Initially at South Burlington and subsequently at the Eco-Park, the Food Group tested John's idea that organic materials otherwise regarded as wastes can be cascaded upward to become higher-value products. Eric worked with materials such as spent brewery wastes and straw used for animal bedding. At the first stage of its metamorphosis, the organic waste was inoculated with fungi. It then served as a substrate to grow delectable oyster mushrooms, which commanded good prices in local restaurants. After three or four mushroom harvests, the fungi transformed the former wastes into a nutritious medium that had two marketable products. Some of it was sold as livestock feed for cattle. Earthworms were introduced into another portion to convert it into vermi-compost (compost enriched with worm castings), thus becoming an even higher-value product. This enriched compost is a near-perfect growing medium in terms of nutrients and minerals, and, during the winter, is ideal for growing salad greens such as mesclun. Eric grew greens until the lettuce crops of local farmers came on the market. The substrate was then bagged and sold as a soil amendment.

Five of South Burlington's Crops

1. Koi in the tank in South Burlington.

2. Tilapia grown in South Burlington.

3. Salad greens in South Burlington.

4. Worms from the Eco-Machine.

5. Oyster mushrooms growing in the South Burlington plant.

No New Alchemy/Ocean Arks project would be complete without fish, of course, and the Food Group espoused this still environmentally sound method of protein production. Eric and his crew raised tilapia and yellow perch, which they sold locally. They retained yet another portion of the substrate used for the mushrooms and worm compost to blend it with aquatic plants to feed to the fish. The ecosystem in which the fish live produced a portion of their food in the form of algae and aquatic plants. In this way, the same organisms that purified the water produced much of the nutrition needed by the fish. Data indicate that this upwardly cascading form of ecological design yields 1 pound of fish flesh from three-quarters of a pound of external feed. This compares favorably with the standard aquaculture ratio of the 1 to 2 pounds of feed needed to produce a pound of fish flesh. The fish, like the off-season salad greens and cut flowers, also found ready local markets. The jury is still out on the full economic potential of this multiuse approach to maximizing local resources. Using an ecosystem model, however, five saleable products—animal feeds, mushrooms, earthworms, mesclun, and a soil amendment—were gleaned from what is normally discarded as waste.

Although still largely ignored by mainstream economics as of this writing, the Food Group unarguably demonstrated that integrated year-round food production is viable. No longer a part of Ocean Arks, the Food Group has joined the Intervale Foundation and is now called the Center for Farm Innovation. It is under the direction of Dr. Guy Roberts, who has expanded the program to include gas production from animal wastes. The wastes are processed in biodigesters or bioreactors utilizing the waste heat from the on-site wood chip–fired electricity-generating plant. The next step at the Eco-Park is to demonstrate this form of ecologically derived economics on a commercial scale. In the winter of 2004, John's students at the University of Vermont designed several models of a twenty-first-century bioshelter for the project. The City of Burlington has offered financial assistance in developing the Eco-Park, possibly within a three-year time frame. Should all this prove successful, the prospects for year-round local food production—with the added bonus of improved food security—as part of an ecologically based economy will be greatly enhanced. Then the Ark concept truly will have come home, fulfilling its promise in "weaving together the sun, wind, biology, and architecture on behalf of humanity."

chapter twelve

The New
Alchemy Legacy

The rule of no realm is mine, but all worthy things that are in
peril as the world now stands, those are my care. And for my
part I shall not wholly fail in my task if anything passes
through this night that can still grow fair or bear fruit in days
to come. For I too am a steward, did you not know?
—J. R. R. Tolkien, *The Return of the King*

The influence of New Alchemy and Ocean Arks continues to germinate
and take root in many forms and in many places. In 1998 its reach took
on a new and unexpected dimension when the School of Natural Resources at the University of Vermont offered John Todd a position as
research professor and distinguished lecturer. Officially referred to as
Ecological Design, his course is really New Alchemy rendered academically respectable. Students learn to think systemically, to see not only
the interconnected reality of the living world, but the need to rethink
and remake the human presence within that context. That this message is being heard is reflected in feedback from the students. One of
John's former students applied this understanding to his senior thesis.
"Ecological design is a rapidly emerging, multi-disciplinary field that
seeks to revolutionize the way in which humans interact with their biotic and abiotic environment," he wrote. "A major emphasis is placed
on research in human behavior. Key to this is the idea of a strong sense
of place and of belonging to the Earth. Humans must seek to reconnect
themselves to the natural environment, foster stewardship, and enhance responsibility."

After John's first semester of teaching, a number of his students
founded an activist group they call CEL, the Consortium for Ecological

Living. CEL's self-appointed mandate is to upgrade the university's environmental performance. From its inception it has proved a vocal and effective catalyst for heightened ecological awareness and action and is a strong presence on campus. Their concern is not only a broader academic acknowledgment of the primacy of ecological issues but also the physical impact of the university on the environment. Like comparable student organizations on other campuses, CEL is demanding that the university reexamine and revise many of its practices and reduce its overall ecological footprint. At the University of Vermont, top-level administration has begun to pay attention.

With the current student body numbering ten thousand, the university is expanding rapidly, concentrating particularly on its business and medical faculties. This has engendered the construction of several new buildings and debate about redesigning existing ones. Fueled by a combination of student activism and concerned faculty, the administration also recognized the environment as a key niche for a Vermont-based institution for higher learning. In the spring of 2004 the Rubenstein School of Environment and Natural Resources held a competition among four competing architectural firms for redesigning its home, the Aiken Building, to achieve improved environmental efficiency. The winning design demonstrated the required ecological, engineering, and architectural elements to produce a "living building that supports the academic community and a diversity of life forms within a surrounding environment that embodies an integration with the natural world." Other initiatives to reduce the ecological footprint of the campus include greening student housing facilities and a new, environmentally designed University Commons Building.

Other educational institutions across the country do not have to reinvent the wheel in the name of state-of-the-art environmental performance. On the campus of Oberlin College, at the instigation of David Orr, Distinguished Professor of Environmental Studies there, is a new building with standards that provide an advanced and successful model for others to emulate. The Adam Joseph Lewis Center used sustainable materials in construction; it maximizes the use of natural light, heating, and cooling; it generates most of its own electricity; and it installed one of John's Eco-Machines to purify the building's wastes. Reflecting the ecosystems of its Ohio setting, the surrounding landscaping includes a small, restored wetland and a forest as well as gardens and orchards.

Like David Orr, John remains mindful that the campus cannot exist as an island unto itself, either socially or politically. To forge awareness of this in Vermont, he is fostering a partnership between the university and Ocean Arks to address the deterioration of the watershed that drains into the Lake Champlain basin. The resulting program is intended to expand the range of ecological design in several new directions. This approach to watershed restoration involves the following:

1. Modifying hydrological cycles on a microscale.
2. Working first upstream then downstream in the watershed.
3. Developing many local points of intervention.
4. Allowing local topography, including buildings, parking lots, and roadways, to direct design.
5. Employing natural systems engineering.
6. Incorporating organisms such as fungi, mosses, and higher plants to sequester metals, bind phosphorus, and destroy pathogens or to break down organic compounds, including petroleum-based products.

Understanding hydrological cycles is key to this onsite approach. In most of the Northeast rainfall descends through dense vegetation and is filtered through the soil before reaching the water table and, eventually, surface waters. The process proceeds gradually and takes time. When rain falls on built environments such as city streets, shopping malls, or parking lots, the hydrological cycle is interrupted. There is no filtering process. Runoff is collected in storm drains and discharged abruptly into local receiving waters. To counter this, designers and engineers will attempt to re-create ecological elements that mimic the function of the forest or the meadow within the built environment. Water collected on rooftops, for example, can be filtered through constructed wetlands or used to irrigate rooftop gardens. Parking lot runoff can be directed through a series of swales or low-lying wetlands between the paved surface and the receiving body of water.

Teams with four kinds of specialized expertise are involved in the Vermont partnership. They include staff and students from the Rubenstein School of Environment and Natural Resources who will analyze the watershed, study processes of local decision making and stakeholder concerns, and look at intervention near pollution sources. The role of Ocean Arks is to help assess and install appropriate bioremediation intervention technological elements. Each watershed has many potential points of intervention. Rather than attempt a single large-scale solution, this plan for watershed rehabilitation will work at the level of the household, farmstead, city block, mall, industrial park, and roadway. Once again, ecological design substitutes information, appropriate technologies, and organisms for costly hardware and engineering.

Ocean Arks is branching off in other new directions as well. With Michael Shaw's resignation as director in 2004, the implementation of the technologies in

North America was passed on to John Todd Research and Design, a consulting company headed by Jonathan Todd. Michael Shaw, through the extensive global network of the Findhorn Association, continued the technology transfer to other parts of the world. This enabled Ocean Arks to focus more exclusively on education, communication, and outreach, nationally and internationally. One of the younger staff members created a new sub-group that reflects this direction. As the Food Group did when it moved on to join forces with the other businesses and organizations in the Burlington Eco-Park, this group, more concerned with Ocean Arks' mandate to serve the water, was launched by staff member Ryan Case. The Water Stewards Network will address water issues on both global and local levels. Ryan was politicized on water issues by the shotgun expansion of the corporatized water industry over the past few years. In coming decades, he realizes, control of water is predicted to become as controversial as control of oil. Transnational water corporations are competing for water technologies, bottled water, and water services. They do so with the support of governments and international financial and development institutions such as the World Bank, the International Monetary Fund, and the World Trade Organization. Globally, enormous dams and unprecedented water transfer schemes are in the making.

To battle corporate control of so essential a resource, Ryan intends the Water Stewards Network to act as a think tank, drawing on leading environmentalists from around the world. Early on he managed to sign on luminaries such as activists Vandana Shiva, Bolivia's José Olivera, and author Lyall Watson to act as advisers. The Water Stewards will collaborate with experts to create flexible multidisciplinary teams that will address specific situations and implement strategies for water stewardship. This is where Ocean Arks' bioremediation techniques and technologies will have a role. We will work with government agencies, non-government organizations, philanthropic foundations, and grassroots organizations to agitate for everyone's right to access to water and to disseminate the knowledge and technologies needed for the protection and conservation of the planet's waters.

Concern for human as well as environmental health has recently forged a direct link with what Rachel Carson called the "infinitely healing" potential of the natural world. In 2003, John met with representatives of the Society for Integrative Medicine. Under discussion was an undeniable trend that is disturbing many doctors and practitioners in the medical community: Cancer rates continue to climb in spite of the billions of dollars being spent in research and treatment. The World Health Organization estimates that 70 percent of cancers are environmentally caused. A number of medical professionals see a parallel between this rise and the number and amount of chemicals seeping into the environment from agriculture, manufacturing, and combustion. Wildlife is equally susceptible to toxified environments.

Many medical people are beginning to recognize the close coupling between human and environmental health, which is why they were interested in talking to John. They concluded that a close-knit alliance between the medical profession and the environmental movement is urgently needed. Such an alliance would draw on the knowledge and research of both sectors to tackle health problems from a holistic perspective. In addition to lobbying for coming to grips with environmental abuses, John has proposed that living ecologies be installed as healing centers in hospitals, convalescent centers, homes for the elderly, halfway houses, and other health care facilities. In the lineage of the Arks, they would be sunlit rooms that mirror the outer world of nature, filled with plants and flowers, tanks of water, and small ponds. Studies confirm that patients with access to some form of nature recover more quickly and have fewer relapses. John's plan would facilitate this by integrating holistically designed systems into the areas where patients are already spending some of their convalescent time. If adopted, this could prove a model that would have a major impact on public attitudes to the natural world. From literally reconnecting human well-being with larger life processes we could learn "something infinitely healing" about ourselves and the planet.

In recognition of his innovative thinking in ecological design, John has received two honorary doctorates and four patents. Two of his patents were for solar-aquatic methods for treating wastewater; the other two were for the invention of ecological fluidized beds. He has also been given a number of awards. In 1999, *Time* magazine named him a "Hero of the Planet." A book published by the Lemelson-MIT program entitled *Inventing Modern America* cited John as one of thirty-five inventors—and the only biologist—who have "contributed to raising human standards of living." The book presents, according to Lester C. Thurow's introduction, "snapshots of the twentieth-century innovation that led us to where we are, and a peek into the torrent of inventiveness that is appearing at the start of the twenty-first century." If ecological design remains a component of that torrent, a transition to a more sustainable world is still a hopeful possibility.

Over the same New Alchemy/Ocean Arks years recounted in this book, from the early 1970s to the present, Bill McLarney and the Asociación ANAI in Costa Rica have achieved a much-heralded model for sustainability on a regional level, one that could be applied to much of the rest of the developing world. According to the Swedish International Development Authority, "ANAI has laid the foundation for a self-sustained and lasting development process at the local level." In spite of extensive road-building and the resultant tourism and commercialization, rural economic development in Talamanca goes hand in hand with the conservation of biodiversity and natural resources, thanks to ANAI. The organization's list of achievements is impressive by anyone's standards. By the early twenty-first century ANAI had been instrumental in establishing a regional biological corridor that stretches from the continental divide to the sea; a national wildlife refuge that is co-managed by government, local communities, and NGOs; a marine turtle conservation program; a cooperative serving a thousand farmers; a regionwide aquatic biomonitoring program with a strong educational component; eight community-based ecotourism ventures that provide a growing source of income for local people; Central America's first raptor migration monitoring program; a regional training center that serves more than two thousand people a year; and an organic agriculture program to preserve small farms.

As a result of such agricultural programs, Talamanca has become the leading producer and exporter of organic crops in Central America. The Talamanca Small Producers Association (APPTA) is a farmer-run group that is the major supplier of organic chocolate to the North American market—all of it from small family farms. Farmers' incomes, in some cases, have tripled. At the World Summit on Sustainable Technology in Johannesburg, South Africa, in 2002, ANAI and its partners in the Talamanca Initiative were awarded the prestigious Equator Prize. Although Bill disclaims any credit, it is not a bad track record for an ornery, fish-loving, mud-slogging gringo and his Costa Rican colleagues and fellow community members.

Through another branch of the New Alchemy legacy, Ty Cashman, Greg Watson, and John Quinney, struggling in the face of the outdated and rapacious energy and environmental policies of the George W. Bush administration, are still engaged on the energy frontline and are inching us closer to an age of renewable energy and a sustainable economy. Educators Kim Knorr and Debbie Habib have also extended their reach. Kim is a leader in the Pennsylvania organic agriculture movement. Debbie and her husband, Rick Baruc, who met at the Farm, have created a replica of New Alchemy in western Massachusetts in the form of the Seeds of Solidarity Education Center, which "provides people of all ages with the inspiration and practical tools to use renewable energy and grow their own food."

Out in the wider world, Christina Rawley and Ron Zweig are the most global of the New Alchemists, framing policy and programs in the international sphere that improve the economies of underserved people, and in Christina's case, particularly women and children in Africa and Asia. Predictably, however, it has been Gary Hirshberg who has taken the tiger by the tail in terms of tackling the realm of money and power. It was always his conviction that we would never create profound change without converting that domain to our way of thinking. Under his leadership, the Stonyfield Farm Yogurt Company has conserved over 13,000 acres of organic dairy farm land in New England. It tithes 10 percent of its profits to help and protect the environment. Not resting on his laurels, Gary remained convinced that unless Stonyfield was influencing the behavior of decision-makers in the world's largest corporations, he was falling short of his goal. In 2001, still adhering strictly to his social and ecological ethic, he negotiated a partnership with the transnational Danon group. His challenge now is to see whether Stonyfield can maintain its standards in the global arena.

Elsewhere the New Alchemy legacy continues to be manifested in almost as many ways as there are New Alchemists and Ocean Arkers to do so. Nowhere is it more directly traceable than back at the Farm itself, now known as Alchemy Farm, and the home of the cohousing community started by Hilde Maingay and Earle Barnhart. Hilde and Earle's beautiful state-of-the-art environmental house adjoins the restored Ark. Around it, exquisitely landscaped by Earle and Hilde, the Farm is very different yet somehow still the same: timeless and peaceful. The present is there, complete in itself. Sometimes, however, I momentarily lapse into a time warp. I seem to hear a faint ghost of women's laughter floating up from the gardens; glimpse sun-browned children racing across the fields; sense for a moment the intensity of weekly meetings and uproarious group feasts; and long to revisit those long-ago golden years. In a more realistic state I am content to know that the alchemy lives on in the place where it all began.

Changing Worldviews

People often ask why, if the knowledge, skills, and technologies for a sustainable world pioneered by New Alchemy and Ocean Arks offer so many solutions to the problems that beset us, they are not more widely applied. It is a tough question. And there are many answers. I sometimes feel boxed into a corner comparable to that of Jungian analyst James Hillman when he wrote his book *We've Had a Hundred Years of Psychotherapy and the World's Getting Worse*. We have been on our quest for alternatives to current destructive practices for more than a generation. And the world *is* getting worse.

In terms of recent history this can be partly explained by the fact that until the early 1990s the reach of the corporate stranglehold on the world economy was somewhat masked by the cold war. When that event so unexpectedly and quickly ended, some of us allowed ourselves to hope that the so-called peace dividend could be redirected toward areas of real need. But the corporations were too adept for us. Already positioned to exploit and despoil in the name of protecting the

Restored Ark with attached solar house.

world from communism, they segued into corporate-managed globalism without losing a beat. Sweeping up politicians and governments in their rising tide, they consolidated their position. Officially sanctioning their power through treaties such as the North American Free Trade Agreement, the General Agreement on Tariffs and Trade, and the Free Trade Agreement of the Americas, the giant transnational corporations formed the Global Trade Organization (GTO) and prepared to rule the world.

So the 1990s swept over us in an all-engulfing wave of economic expansion, free trade, and corporate takeover. Events moved swiftly, and often beyond public scrutiny. It was not until the end of the decade that widespread resistance became sufficiently organized to confront the emergent reality. Anticipating this dynamic, Theodore Roszak, in his book *Person/Planet*, had asked, "What then does the Earth do? She begins to speak to something in us—an ideal of life, a sense of identity—that has until now been harbored within only an eccentric and marginal few. And the cry of pain which that generation utters is the planet's own personal cry for rescue, her protest against the bigness of things becoming ours."

That cry of pain erupted into a roar in Seattle in the late fall of 1999. It took the form of vehement protest against the meeting of the GTO there. And it was heard

Interior of restored Ark.

around the world. It continued to echo in Washington, D.C., Thailand, Melbourne, Prague, Quebec City, Genoa, and New York. Silenced for a while by the tragedy of September 11, 2001, lest it be confused with terrorist causes, it is again rallying those who struggle for a sustainable world. In 2003 the movement swelled again in worldwide protest against the Bush administration's war in Iraq. Author Jonathan Schell said of the huge international rally on February 15 of that year, "On that day, history may one day record, global democracy was born."

Beyond the machinations of national and corporate agendas and the abyss that terrorism has opened in our collective life, one truth remains nonnegotiable: The destiny of everyone is irrevocably interdependent, interconnected, and inter-woven with that of Earth and its innumerable and irreplaceable life-forms. The way we live now is predicated on an outmoded understanding of the world. A shift from our inherited Newtonian/Cartesian acceptance of the natural world as mechanistic and malleable at will to human manipulation to a Gaian cosmology is a vast leap of mind—and heart. This constitutes a change of mind-set—of worldview—as profound as any in the past. Yet, as Einstein once pointed out, only when we change the way we think will we change the way we behave.

One analogy often cited for the phase we have now entered is that of an ocean liner moving at full speed. Should a change of course be required, the first step is to reduce momentum. Such a slowdown could well be under way. The world economy is uncertain at best. The Enron and subsequent scandals exposed the underbelly of corporate ruthlessness and government compliance. Living in a world of escalating terrorism has revealed the vulnerability of our sprawling global and national life-support systems in terms of food, energy, transportation, and distribution networks. The strongest hope for not only a sustainable but a more secure world argues for what Theodore Roszak called "alternatives to person-and-planet colossalism." Regional and community levels of food and energy production and local industries provide few targets of much interest to those who would harm us.

Environmental, economic, and now security factors argue for the inherent good sense of more sustainable practices. This transition need not be overwhelmingly difficult. Many of the components to facilitate it are well in place, serving as signposts to guide us. In the conflict-ridden area of religion, ecologist and theologian Thomas Berry maintains that scientific/poetic awe of the forces that brought the world and the universe into being could serve as a universal and unifying template upon which people and cultures can graft their traditional spiritual beliefs. A Gaian worldview holds all life to be a sacred ecology in which humankind serves as steward.

John and I have been blessed to have been led to such an understanding. We have been blessed, too, in that pending environmental disaster has been kept at bay for much of our children's lives. They have been granted their chance to grow into themselves and find their place in the world, to marry and take responsibility for another generation. But what of their children? What kind of world will they inherit? If there is no radical shift from our present course, the disaster I feared so long ago looms larger and closer. Yet thanks to a large measure to the tireless efforts of Al Gore, it still need not happen. There are many reasons to see a transition to a sustainable world as already well begun.

In spite of the last-gasp hegemony of ruthless oil cartels, wind power is growing at 30 percent a year. In a few years solar energy in the form of photovoltaics and fuel cells could be widely employed to power buildings and electric cars. New inventions in generating hydroelectricity with small, environmentally benign generators, such as the Gorlov rotor, are proving even more cost effective than wind. The organic food market is expanding at a rate of 20 percent a year in North America and 30 percent in Europe, and the struggle has shifted to supporting small, local growers from corporations geared to seize their market niche. Organic growers and consumers are also leaders in the struggle against a takeover of food crops by genetic engineering. According to Lester Brown of the Worldwatch Institute, there are even chinks within corporate structures, including several of the oil and car companies. In late 2002, one of General Motors' vice presidents for research and design announced on National Public Radio that the time was ripe for reinventing the world energy structure.

The scientific foundation for sustainable cultures demands, as Wade Green said so many years ago of New Alchemy, cooking up a gentle science of survival. According to Dr. Mae-Wan Ho of England's Open University, "The mechanistic view is rapidly losing ground within contemporary Western science. An organic revolution is sweeping across the disciplines from quantum physics to the ecology of complexity and molecular genetics." As an outpost of that organic revolution, New Alchemy, it should be remembered, was originally forged in the form of a question. At that time we truly did not know whether it would prove possible for people to provide for their basic needs sustainably while healing the injuries we have inflicted on the planet. As early as the mid-1970s, from our research and experimentation in food production, renewable energy, and integration of function, we became convinced that to do so was both feasible and doable. That remains as viable now as it was then.

Through the work at Ocean Arks and that of thousands of others, we now know not only *that* we can create a sustainable world, we know *how* to do it. In terms of ecological design we may still be at the Model T stage, but the potential is exponential. The thinking that guided the work at New Alchemy and Ocean Arks has begun to penetrate scientific, academic, and, occasionally, corporate fields. From time to time it finds a voice in the media. It is a strong part of the platform of the antiglobalization movement. Slowly, it is informing Earth's stewards.

Bill McLarney is still probably the most quotable of the New Alchemists when it comes to encapsulating what might have been called our philosophy. His most succinct summation dates back to a sultry August evening long ago when a cluster of us were sitting in a circle on the grass for a group interview. A microphone, artfully hidden by a bouquet of marigolds, had been placed at the center of the group. We were being asked what role we, as New Alchemists, could play in events of the larger world. When Bill's turn came, he concealed his beer can, squinted into the camera, and, in a few words, managed to summarize what many of us were feeling: "Well, I don't suppose any of us should be fool enough to think that we can save the world. But if each of us were to look at some of the directions we'd like to see it go in, then put our own little bit of force behind them—and have a hell of a good time while we're doing it—then that's what we should do."

Well, we did. And we are. And we plan to go on doing so.

Please join us. There are far more of us now. And new generations are coming on board. We have everything to gain and nothing to lose. Authorities ranging from Native American leaders to Nobel Prize winners agree that it is not too late, but that we must act promptly and decisively. Author and environmental activist Paul Hawken maintains that the adherents of sustainability will prevail because the empirical truth of our understanding of the planet's finite life-support systems continues to prove itself. John Todd estimates that restructuring present cultures to adapt to the tenets of sustainability could reduce the ecological footprint of humanity on the planet by as much as 90 percent. Writing of the part of each of us as individuals in such a transformation, Thomas Berry claimed in *The Great Work*, "We were chosen by some power beyond ourselves for this historical task. We do not choose the moment of our birth, who our parents will be, our particular culture, or the historical moment when we will be born. The nobility of our lives, however, depends upon the manner in which we come to understand and fulfill our assigned role."

Sometimes it takes a shock as profound as the environmental crisis we now face to jolt us into understanding what we stand to lose. Our heart-stoppingly beautiful home planet, suspended and palpably alive in the vast darkness of space, is, as far as we know, unique. And if a handful of people who called themselves New Alchemists and Ocean Arkers could learn what has to be done to protect and restore Earth, it does not take an enormous leap of faith to imagine what could happen if communities, states, countries, and international alliances were to dedicate themselves to working on behalf of the life of the planet.

Our early mentor Gregory Bateson once observed that many of us "have lost that sense of unity of biosphere and humanity that would bind and reassure us all with an affirmation of beauty." When we view the rest of planetary life as separate and apart from ourselves, the inclination is to strive, as we now do, for domination and control. On the other hand, a worldview arising from a renewed awareness of the interconnectedness of all life draws us toward engagement and participation. From such a connection arises a sense of belonging—of belonging to community, to the human family, and to the living Earth. It is, perhaps, the source of what Wendell Berry has called "the courage for love."

Bibliography

Annals of Earth, Ocean Arks International, Falmouth, MA.

Ausubel, Kenny, with J. P. Harpingnies. *Nature's Operating Instructions: The True Biotechnologies*. San Francisco: Sierra Club Books, 2004.

Bardach, John E., John Ryther, and William O. McLarney. *Aquaculture: The Farming and Husbandry of Freshwater and Marine Organisms*. New York: John Wiley and Sons, 1972.

Bateson, Gregory. *Steps to an Ecology of Mind: Collected Essays in Anthropology, Psychiatry, Evolution, and Epistemology*. San Francisco: Chandler, 1972.

Benello, C. George, Robert Swann, and Shann Turnbull. *Building Sustainable Communities: Tools and Concepts for Self-Reliant Economic Change*. New York: Bootstrap Press, 1989.

Benyus, Janine M. *Biomimicry: Innovation Inspired by Nature*. New York: William Morrow, 1997.

Berry, Thomas. *The Great Work: Our Way into the Future*. New York: Bell Tower, 1999.

Berry, Wendell. *Life Is a Miracle: An Essay Against Modern Superstition*. New York: Counterpoint, 2000.

Brown, Lester R. *Eco-Economy: Building an Economy for the Earth*. New York: W. W. Norton & Company, 2001.

Capra, Fritjof. *The Web of Life: A New Scientific Understanding of Living Systems*. New York: Anchor Books Doubleday, 1996.

Carson, Rachel. *The Sense of Wonder*. New York and Evanston: Harper & Row, 1956.

Girardet, Herbert. *Creating Sustainable Cities*. Dartington, England: Green Books, 1999.

Hannum, Hildegarde. *People, Land, and Community: Collected E. F. Schumacher Lectures*. New Haven, CT: Yale University Press, 1997.

Hawken, Paul, Amory Lovins, and L. Hunter Lovins. *Natural Capitalism: Creating the Next Industrial Revolution*. Boston, New York, London: Little, Brown, 1999.

Hemenway, Toby. *Gaia's Garden: A Guide to Home-Scale Permaculture*. White River Junction, VT: Chelsea Green, 2001.

Jacobs, Jane. *The Nature of Economies*. New York: The Modern Library, 2000.

Kangas, Patrick C. *Ecological Engineering: Principles and Practice*. Boca Raton, FL: Lewis Publishers, 2004.

Kellert, Stephen R., and Edward O. Wilson. *The Biophilia Hypothesis*. Washington, DC: Island Press/Shearwater Books, 1993.

Lappé, Frances Moore, and Anna Lappé. *Hope's Edge: The Next Diet for a Small Planet*. New York: Jeremy P. Tarcher/Putnam, 2002.

Lovelock, James. *Healing Gaia: Practical Medicine for the Planet*. New York: Harmony Books, 1991.

McKibben, Bill. *Hope, Human and Wild: True Stories of Living Lightly on the Earth*. St. Paul, MN: Hungry Mind Press, 1995.

Meis, Maria, and Vandana Shiva. *Ecofeminism*. Halifax: Fernwood Publications; London: Zed Books, 1993.

Merrill, Richard, editor. *Radical Agriculture*. New York: Harper & Row. A Harper Colophon Book, 1976.

Mills, Stephanie, editor. *Turning Away from Technology: A New Vision for the 21st Century*. San Francisco: Sierra Club Books, 1997.

Nestle, Marion. *Food Politics: How the Food Industry Influences Nutrition and Health*. Berkeley: University of California Press, 2002.

Petrini, Carlo, editor. *Slow Food: Collected Thoughts on Taste, Tradition and the Honest Pleasures of Food*. White River Junction, VT: Chelsea Green, 2001.

Orr, David W. *Earth in Mind*. Washington, DC: Island Press, 1994.

———. *The Last Refuge: Patriotism, Politics, and the Environment in an Age of Terror*. Washington, DC: Island Press, 2004.

———. *The Nature of Design: Ecology, Culture, and Human Intention*. Oxford: Oxford University Press, 2002.

Roszak, Theodore, Mary E. Gomes, and Allen D. Kanner. *Ecopsychology: Restoring the Earth, Healing the Mind*. San Francisco: Sierra Club Books, 1995.

Schumacher, E. F. *Small Is Beautiful: Economics As If People Mattered*. Point Roberts, WA: Hartley & Marks, 1999.

Todd, Nancy Jack, and John Todd. *From Eco-Cities to Living Machines: Principles of Ecological Design*. Berkeley: North Atlantic Books, 1993.

Todd, John, and Nancy Jack Todd. *Tomorrow Is Our Permanent Address: The Search for an Ecological Science of Design as Embodied in the Bioshelter*. New York: Harper & Row, 1980.

Van der Ryn, Sim, and Stuart Cowan. *Ecological Design*. Washington, DC: Island Press, 1996.

Index